2,—

Dining
in
HISTORIC
KENTUCKY

A Restaurant Guide With Recipes

by Marty Godbey

Illustrations by James Asher

McClanahan
Publishing House

Library of Congress Catalog Card Number: 90 066916
International Standard Book Number: 0-913383-18-X
Cover photograph: The Mansion at Griffin Gate, Lexington, Kentucky

Illustrations by James Asher
Back cover photograph by Frank Godbey
Cover design and book layout by James Asher

Manufactured in the United States of America

All book order correspondence should be addressed to:
McClanahan Publishing House, Inc.
P. O. Box 100
Kuttawa, Kentucky 42055
(502)388-9388
1-800-544-6959

INTRODUCTION

Kentucky's talent for hospitality is renowned: from the time when a frontier traveler in the wilderness was welcomed to a crossroads tavern, great pride has been taken in the foods offered to guests. Even under conditions of poverty, the best the house has to offer is set forth; in times of plenty, polished walnut and cherry tables reflect silver laden with delicacies, and visitors are pressed to indulge themselves.

The finest of locally available ingredients has always been used here, whether wild mint is blended with a beverage made of limestone water and homegrown corn, or mahogany-colored "old" ham is sandwiched in crisp beaten biscuits, or tender young chickens are fried golden brown. A tradition of good food carefully prepared and graciously served has been carried on for generations.

To Kentuckians, history is as much a part of daily life as is food— roads and buildings known by Daniel Boone, George Rogers Clark, and Abraham Lincoln not only remain, they are frequently still in use, cherished for their indirect contribution to the Commonwealth and the Nation.

A few establishments that provided food and lodging for these and other early Kentuckians are still in business; many other buildings of historic significance have been restored or refurbished and converted into restaurants. Hotels, lodge halls, and a theatre are again places to congregate; office workers lunch in business structures where their counterparts worked in the past; and homes are thrown open to guests.

Train stations, schools, a general store, and a warehouse have been adapted as restaurants, preserving their unique qualities and offering patrons a little history with their food.

Such unlikely structures as churches, a bank, a fire house, and a tow boat have been successfully converted to restaurants, giving visitors an opportunity to observe at first hand some of the places their ancestors took for granted.

There are no two alike, and because they belong to people who value the past enough to utilize old buildings, with the attendant inconveniences, they are all very special places.

Although the buildings are old, the food reflects current tastes and interests. Kentucky fare today is more diversified than might be suspected— traditional regional favorites are joined by innovative methods of preparation and products new to the area. Ready availability of fresh seafoods has been an important influence, as has an awareness of diet and nutrition in today's restaurant-goers. And Kentucky's ethnic mix has contributed new delights to an already rich and varied list.

A visit to any of Kentucky's restaurants in historic buildings is well repaid, for an appreciation of the past is as easily absorbed as the excellent food, and the diner leaves satisfied in more ways than one.

Using *DINING IN HISTORIC KENTUCKY* as a Travel Guide

Dining In Historic Kentucky s a complete revision of the book which first appeared in 1985. Its success prompted *Dining In Historic Ohio, Dining In Historic Tennessee,* and *Dining In The Historic South,* all based on accumulated notes about restaurants in historic buildings. Gathered from advertisements, history books, old travel guides, word-of-mouth reports, and personal experience, these notes grew into computer files, and then books.

The same criteria were used in compiling this revision as in all previous books: restaurants were chosen on a basis of historic, architectural, and culinary interest (frequently all three) coupled with business stability. There are twenty restaurants in the revised *Dining In Historic Kentucky* that did not appear in the original; new restaurants in restored buildings indicate increased public awareness of historic preservation, and their success proves the validity of the concept.

Kentucky's tradition of hospitality, carried out in her restaurants, made selection difficult; ultimately, choices were made on preservation/restoration grounds. Of the 48 buildings which house the restaurants included, 35 are on the National Register of Historic Places; one is a National Historic Landmark. In addition, those chosen all met the final requirement: they are places a first-time visitor would describe enthusiastically to friends.

The author, often with companions, ate anonymously in every restaurant included, to ensure the same treatment any hungry traveler might receive. No restaurant paid to be included or was told of the project until asked to participate. Restaurant owners and managers have been enthusiastic, gracious, and cooperative, some providing recipes that had never before been disclosed.

As an aid to travelers, restaurants are listed roughly east to west; resource information between text and recipes provides addresses and telephone numbers, and all travelers are encouraged to call before driving long distances.

Laws governing the sale of alcoholic beverages vary greatly. If beverages are available, it will be so indicated in the resource information; many dry areas permit "brown-bagging," or bringing your own, but it would be wise to inquire ahead.

Symbols used for brevity include charge card references: AE= American Express, CB= Carte Blanche, DC= Diner's Club, DS= Discover, JCB= Japan Credit Bureau, MC= Master Card, V= Visa.

Most of these restaurants would fall into the "moderate" category of expensiveness; an effort was made to include all price ranges. Using entree prices as a gauge, dollar signs ($) are used to indicate reasonable ($), moderate ($$), and more expensive ($$$). Luncheon prices are usually significantly lower, and the amount spent in any restaurant is increased by the "extras" ordered, i.e., appetizers, drinks, and side orders.

None of these restaurants would be considered expensive by East or West Coast standards; if cost is a determining factor, however, most restaurants will gladly provide a price range over the telephone.

Visitors are cautioned that some of the restaurants in *Dining In Historic Kentucky* have a large local following, and their busy seasons may be determined by such events as The Kentucky Derby (first Saturday in May) not familiar to non-residents. To avoid disappointment, CALL AHEAD FOR RESERVATIONS.

TABLE OF CONTENTS

Dining in Historic
KENTUCKY

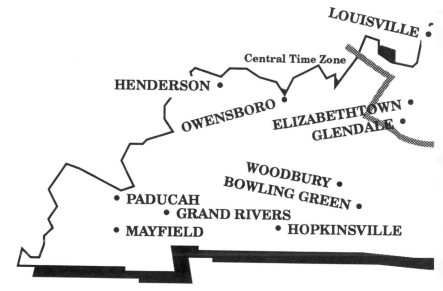

LOUISVILLE

Central Time Zone

HENDERSON •

OWENSBORO •

ELIZABETHTOWN •
GLENDALE •

WOODBURY •
BOWLING GREEN •

• PADUCAH
• GRAND RIVERS
• MAYFIELD   • HOPKINSVILLE

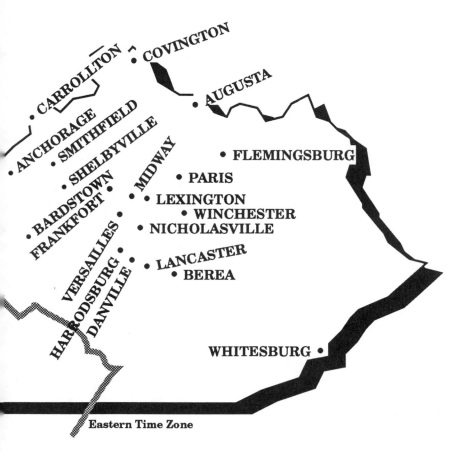

CARROLLTON
COVINGTON
AUGUSTA
ANCHORAGE
SMITHFIELD
SHELBYVILLE
MIDWAY
FLEMINGSBURG
BARDSTOWN
PARIS
FRANKFORT
LEXINGTON
WINCHESTER
NICHOLASVILLE
VERSAILLES
HARRODSBURG
LANCASTER
DANVILLE
BEREA
WHITESBURG

Eastern Time Zone

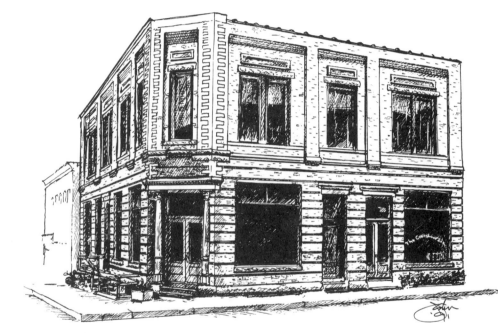

THE COURTHOUSE CAFÉ
Whitesburg

Dr. Thomas Walker discovered coal on Pine Mountain in 1750, but when Letcher County was formed in 1842, it was not yet being mined. Isolated by its rugged terrain, the county was sparsely populated, and Whitesburgh (the "h" was dropped in 1892), chosen as county seat, was a village of two churches, one school, three stores, one tavern, and less than fifty inhabitants.

Letcher's small farms produced hogs, cattle, horses, and wool; ginseng, harvested from the woods for medicinal purposes, was an important cash crop. By the 1880s and 1890s, quantities of timber were felled and floated down the Kentucky and Cumberland rivers.

Whitesburg, its people, and environs are believed to have inspired the stories of Kentucky author John Fox, Jr., who wrote eleven novels about the Kentucky mountains and the Bluegrass region between 1893 and 1919. Seldom read today outside Kentucky, *The Little Shepherd of Kingdom Come, The Trail of the Lonesome Pine, and Christmas Eve on Lonesome* were enormously popular in their day. These books spread romantic and often erroneous notions about feuds, suspicion, and illegal whiskey operations in the Kentucky mountains.

The railroad reached Whitesburg in 1912, connecting the mountains with the industrial world, and making possible both mining and shipping of coal. The resulting boom spurred establishment of new businesses, one of which was a bank built diagonally across from the courthouse in 1914.

The bank failed within two years, and the two-story red brick building was used for other purposes. At various times, it housed a tavern, a barber shop, law offices, the bus station, and the Whitesburg High School.

In 1969, when Letcher County's blue courthouse was new, Josephine D'Amato Richardson and her husband came to Whitesburg from New Haven, Connecticut, with a grant to train young people in film making. The classes they began eventually expanded to become Apalshop, a complete multi-media workshop.

Intending to stay six months, the Richardsons made Whitesburg their home, and Josephine opened a crafts shop and bookstore in the former bank's corner store. When attorneys with offices upstairs wanted the corner entrance, she negotiated for the rest of the downstairs space, and, with

13

Laura Schuster, opened a restaurant in 1985. Books and crafts were phased out, but lovely quilts still adorn the exposed-brick walls, warming and softening The Courthouse Café.

Pressed-tin ceilings are far above narrow-boarded floors, with light streaming into the L-shaped restaurant from two exposures; at night candles join fresh flowers on each table. The café's food blends Laura's Appalachian heritage with Josephine's Italian background—and it works beautifully.

They provide five lunch specials daily, based on seasonal fresh foods: pastas, salads, a "meat and potatoes" choice, and a vegetarian dish, plus homemade soups and sandwiches. In the evening, you can count on grilled chicken breasts, prepared differently each time; New York strip steaks; perhaps grilled rainbow trout; and cheese ravioli with fresh tomato sauce. Berries, corn, and peas are obtained locally, servings are generous, and the freshness and flavor of each item is paramount.

Desserts, fresh every day, might be Fruit Strudel, Tanglewood Pie (bananas, whipped cream, cream cheese, blueberry topping), or Butterscotch or Chocolate Fudge brownies, topped with ice cream and drizzled with the appropriate sauce.

The Courthouse Café, 104 North Webb Avenue, Whitesburg, is on the corner of Main Street. It is open Monday through Friday, 10 a.m. to 8:30 p.m., with continuous service. Whitesburg is about 32 miles southeast of Hazard, 12 miles from Jenkins at the Virginia border. (606)633-5859. Dress is casual, and reservations are accepted but not necessary. MC,V, personal checks. ($$)

COURTHOUSE CAFÉ
HERBED TOMATO SOUP

1/2 onion,
  finely chopped
Oil for sautéeing
4 cups tomato sauce
4 cups chicken stock
1 Tablespoon
  chopped parsley

1 Tablespoon
  chopped basil leaves
1 Tablespoon
  crushed dried thyme
Salt and pepper

In large saucepan, sauté onion in oil until transparent. Add tomato sauce and stock and bring to a boil; turn off heat and add herbs, salt and pepper. Serves 8.

COURTHOUSE CAFÉ PASTA PRIMAVERA

1 pound fettuccine,
  cooked al denté
2 cloves garlic, diced
1 onion, diced
2 cups diced carrots
Olive oil for sautéeing
2 cups broccoli florets
2 cups sliced zucchini

1 cup sliced mushrooms
2 cups heavy cream
1/2 cup grated
  Parmesan cheese
2 cups diced
  fresh tomato
Salt and pepper

In very large skillet or saucepan, sauté garlic, onion, and carrots in oil 5 minutes. Add broccoli and zucchini and sauté 5 minutes, then add mushrooms. Combine cream and cheese and add to vegetables; add diced tomato and heat through. Season to taste; serve over hot fettuccine. Serves 8 to 10.

COURTHOUSE CAFÉ
STRAWBERRY CREAM PIE

9-inch
  baked pie shell
8 ounces cream cheese,
  softened
1/2 cup sugar

2 Tablespoons milk
1 teaspoon
  almond extract
Fresh strawberries
Strawberry jam

In bowl of electric mixer, blend cream cheese with next 3 ingredients. Spread mixture in pie shell. Hull fresh strawberries and place upside down in circular pattern on top of cream cheese. Warm jam just enough to melt it; brush over strawberries and chill. Serves 8.

THE DEPOT
Flemingsburg

$\mathbf{T}$he Commonwealth of Kentucky began as Kentucky County, Virginia; it was divided into Fayette, Lincoln, and Jefferson counties in 1780, and by 1792, when Kentucky became a separate state, subdivided into nine counties. The state was split into smaller and smaller counties, as many rural Kentuckians believed the size of a county should allow any citizen to ride to the county seat and return home the same day.

The county court was essential to the business of nearly everyone, and Court Monday, scheduled by a statute enacted by the General Assembly, occurred at the county seat on a specified Monday of the month in each county. Hundreds of people attended Court Day, not only for court transactions, but to trade horses, dogs, guns, and other pioneer necessities. Peddlers traveled from one county seat to another, timing their arrival with the Court Day crowds.

Autumn Court Days gave farmers an opportunity to sell their harvest and a chance to visit neighbors before bad weather. In a few counties, the custom of a fall Court Day still stands, and Maysville, Mount Sterling, and Flemingsburg each hold an entire weekend of festivities in conjunction with their Court Days. Streets turn into open markets, with booths of antiques, regional foods, entertainment, and flea market items of every kind. People come from many surrounding counties to participate, as court activities are now a minor part of the proceedings.

Court Day in Flemingsburg is the first weekend in October.

The Depot Restaurant in Flemingsburg occupies a charming railroad station notable for flared weatherboarding and a molded tile roof. It was erected in 1908 to service a narrow-gauge line connecting Flemingsburg with the Louisville and Nashville Railroad. Chartered in 1870 as the Covington, Flemingsburg and Pound Gap Railway, the 17-mile line was operated under numerous names and partnerships during its 79 years of existence. The last train ran December 6, 1955.

The former depot, used for a time by a dairy supply business, was bought by the City of Flemingsburg in 1978 and restored. It opened as a restaurant in 1984, and was placed on the National Register in 1985. Fresh and clean in its gray paint, The Depot still maintains a comfortable waiting-room feeling. In several dining rooms, booths along the walls enhance the railroad theme.

Since January of 1986, it has been operated by Larry and Diane Farris, who provide something different every day—Friday is Prime Rib night, and there's an all-you-can-eat fried cod special all day every Saturday, with hush puppies and sides of french fries, baked beans, or coleslaw. Their extra-good fried country ham is always on the menu, with steaks and a wide assortment of sandwiches. All dinners come with homemade soups (the vegetable is famous) and salad bar.

On weekends, there are peach, apple, and cherry cobblers and through the week, hot fudge sundaes, Brownie Express or rich pecan pie are a great end to an excursion to Flemingsburg.

The Depot, Electric Avenue, Flemingsburg, is just off Main Cross Street, and is open Wednesday, Thursday, and Sunday 11 a.m. to 8 p.m., with continuous service. Friday and Saturday hours are 11 a.m. to 9 p.m. (606)845-0701. Dress is casual, and reservations are accepted (except Mothers' Day) but not necessary. The restaurant is closed on Court Day and the week of July 4th. MC,V, personal checks. ($)

THE DEPOT CREAM OF BROCCOLI SOUP

2 ounces margarine
1/2 cup flour
2 quarts milk
1 1/4 cups shredded
   cheddar cheese

1/2 pound chopped fresh
   or frozen broccoli
Salt and pepper

In large saucepan, melt margarine and stir in flour until smooth. Over medium heat, add milk, stirring often until thickened. Add cheese, stirring until melted, then broccoli. Heat through, season to taste, and serve. Yields about 8 servings.

THE DEPOT CHERRY COBBLER

4 ounces margarine
1 1/2 cups self-rising flour
1 1/2 cups sugar
1 1/2 cups milk
Two 20-ounce cans
cherry pie filling

In 325 degree oven, melt margarine in 9" x 13" pan. In bowl, mix flour and sugar, and stir in milk until blended. When margarine is melted, remove pan from oven and pour batter onto butter. DO NOT STIR. Gently spoon pie filling onto batter. Bake at 325 degrees about 45 minutes. Serves 10 to 12.

THE DEPOT BROWNIE EXPRESS

For each serving:
1 brownie
1 scoop
   vanilla ice cream
1 ounce
   hot fudge topping
Whipped cream

Heat brownie in microwave 30 seconds. Place on saucer with ice cream and hot fudge. Garnish with whipped cream.

THE BEEHIVE TAVERN
Augusta

Captain Philip Buckner, who served as Virginia Commissary Officer during the American Revolution, donated 600 acres from one of his many land grants, and laid out a town along the Ohio River about 1795.

Attracted by flat land and fertile soil, settlers flocked to Augusta in 1797, a year after the county was named for colorful Indian fighter William Bracken.

A ferryboat across the Ohio in 1800 increased the importance of the community, as did the natural harbor at the mouth of Bracken Creek. As a distribution center for goods delivered by steamboat, Augusta prospered in the early Nineteenth Century. Its well-to-do citizens built handsome homes overlooking the River on Water Street (now River Side Drive).

Augusta College, the first Methodist college in the world, was established in 1822, drawing students from nearby states, and by1840, Augusta had achieved a population of 1200, despite loss of the county seat to Brooksville.

In mid-century, railroads began to take commerce away from towns dependant upon steamboat trade. A second blow was delivered to Augusta during the War Between the States, when Southerners removed their sons from the strongly Unionist college, and Northerners were reluctant to send theirs south to school. The town was damaged during a Confederate raid in 1862, and subsequent floods forced many people to move.

Augusta had an interesting agricultural "boom" in the 1870s, when German immigrants, noting the similarity of nearby soil to that in European wine-producing areas, established vineyards. For a few years, Bracken county produced over 30,000 gallons annually, half the national production .

At the corner of Main Street (formerly Upper) and River Side Drive, a two-story Federal-style brick building at the end of a series of rowhouses was built as an apothecary shop and store, possibly as early as 1796, by James Armstrong. Facing the ferry landing, the building, with its lengthy rear extension, was a hotel, later a bank. For many years there was an entrance under the stone lintel facing the corner.

Today, that door is framed in, creating the big corner window in the main dining room of The Beehive Tavern. Its handsome woodwork painted a soft teal, the tavern is decorated with period antiques and, with its enclosed bar in the corner, has the feeling of an eighteenth-century tavern. As part of the Water Street/River Side Drive Historic District, it was placed on the National Register in 1975.

Produced by Chef/owner Luciano (Shawn) Moral, the Beehive's food reflects his Cuban heritage and classical training. Menus change every two weeks, but always feature steaks, prime rib, and his superb black bean soup, and might contain such European classics as Veal Bourguignon or Wiener Schnitzel.

A flawlessly prepared fresh Catch of the Day, a tasty, unusual chicken dish, and homey favorites such as Roast Pork with Fried Apples provide plenty of variety. Salads are crisp and tasty, bread is warm and chewy, and if you can resist a marvelous Caramel Flan, there's always New York Style Cheesecake; rich, dense Chocolate Mousse; and a surprise—recently, a creamy, delicate Trifle Cake dripping with blueberries and impossible to forget.

The Beehive Tavern, 101 West Riverside Drive, Augusta, is open Wednesday through Saturday for lunch, 12 noon to 2 p.m.; dinner, 5 p.m. until closing. Sunday dinner is 12:30 p.m. to 6:30 p.m. Shorter hours prevail in winter. Augusta is 18 miles west of Maysville on the Ohio River. (606)756-2202. All legal beverages are available (except Sunday), dress is casual, and reservations are suggested. Busiest times are during the Sternwheeler Regatta in June, and Heritage Days, Labor Day Weekend. MC,V. ($$)

BEEHIVE TAVERN
CUBAN BLACK BEAN SOUP

2 pounds black beans	1 Tablespoon oregano
4 quarts water	6 cloves garlic, minced
4 bay leaves	2 Tablespoons vinegar
1 cup olive oil	Salt and pepper
1 onion, chopped	2 placeros peppers
2 sweet green peppers,	(optional)
chopped	1 teaspoon hot sauce
Small bunch cilantro,	2 cups dry, imported
chopped	sherry wine
1 Tablespoon cumin	

In large pot, boil beans, water and bay leaves at least 1 hour, or until beans are tender, stirring occasionally to keep from scorching. In a second pot, combine remaining ingredients (except sherry) and cook until vegetables are translucent. Add this to cooked beans and simmer 30 minutes. Add sherry and simmer another 15 minutes. Yields about 16 serv ings.

BEEHIVE TAVERN FISH FRITTERS

1 pound finely
   chopped fish (cod,
   hoagy, or whitefish)
1 onion, chopped
1/2 sweet green pepper,
   chopped
2 eggs

4 Tablespoons milk
4 Tablespoons flour
1 teaspoon ground cumin
1 teaspoon hot pepper
   flakes
Oil for frying

In large bowl, mix all ingredients. Spoon dollops into shallow pan of hot oil and flatten slightly. Cook until golden brown on both sides.

BEEHIVE TAVERN CHICKEN WITH OLIVES

4 boneless chicken
   breast halves,
   skin removed
Flour for dredging
1/2 cup olive oil
2 cloves garlic, minced
1 Tablespoon
   chopped onion

1 teaspoon oregano
Salt
Juice of 1/2 lemon
2 cups dry white wine
1/2 cup black olives
1/2 cup green olives
1 Tablespoon capers

Lightly pound chicken and dredge in flour. Sauté in oil over medium-high heat until lightly browned. Add next 6 ingredients and reduce to simmer. Add olives and capers, and reduce by 1/2. Serves 4.

THE ENGINE HOUSE DELI
Winchester

Clark County, created in 1792, was named for General George Rogers Clark, hero of the Northwest Territory. That same year, the county seat was laid out by a man named Baker, originally from Winchester, Virginia, who named the new town for his old home.

Winchester's economy was based on agriculture until the 1870s, when railroads made it a distribution center. Timber, iron ore, and coal from the mountains were shipped to Winchester and forwarded east to New York, west to Chicago, or to points north and south on the Louisville and Nashville Railroad.

This was the period of Winchester's greatest growth. Between 1865 and 1890, the population increased by more than 7,000 people, and the downtown business district was developed, with many fine Italianate commercial buildings. These structures have changed little, and represent one of the best-preserved and most attractive nineteenth-century commercial districts in Kentucky.

Winchester was incorporated as a city in 1877, the year construction began on the Opera House and its first Fire Hall. In 1885, Fire Chief W. A. Attersal deeded to the city Board of Councilmen a parcel of land on Fairfax Street (now Lexington Avenue) for an Engine House.

The Sanborn Map of 1886 shows a "Steam Engine House and Mayor's office" at 104 Fairfax. Also new was a Silsby Steam Engine, with a capacity of 400 gallons per minute. Reference is made in the 1889 city directory to the "elegant two-story building with pressed-brick front and stone trimmings. In it is an elegantly furnished room containing a library of over 800 volumes contributed by the citizens." Was this Winchester's first public library?

A fire in 1909 destroyed the rear of the Engine House (including the bell tower used to summon volunteer firemen) and part of its second floor; from that time until the completion of the new City Hall in 1915, the engine company was quartered in a temporary home behind the Courthouse.

The former engine house was repaired, and served as home and office for a doctor until about 1920; after that, it was an insurance office, a dry cleaners, and a "blue plate" restaurant during the depression. Later, it housed the Soil Conservation office and a telephone training office, and was briefly a high school hangout in the 1950s. As part of the

Winchester Downtown Commercial District, it was placed on the National Register in 1982.

Occasionally, unfortunate remodeling destroyed part of the building's character, but Bob and Lisa Tabor, who bought it in 1983, have been gradually restoring it, while operating a friendly, casual restaurant that provides some outstanding food and interesting artifacts to enjoy while you eat.

With a lunch counter, tables grouped around a wood stove, and an area in the rear where teenagers are allowed to write on the walls, the Engine House Deli is comfortable for all ages—small children are welcome, and enjoy the couch made of a Victorian bathtub, and the cards and checkers ready for their use.

Chili, made from a famous local recipe, is offered every day, with other soups that change daily; you can build your own "designer sub" or find three friends to share an 18-inch long, pound-and-a-half "Hook and Ladder" sub; square Sicilian-style pizzas have whole wheat crusts and white Cheddar topping; and chilled shrimp with cocktail sauce are boiled in beer, using Paul Prudhomme's method.

There are salads with homemade dressings; sandwiches on homemade bread (made from a potato-dough recipe from the 1940s); a superb Kentucky Hot Brown with "Country Mornay Sauce" (including country sausage and secret ingredients); for dessert, perhaps Chocolate Cheesecake with Oreo™ Cookie Crust, authentic Spumoni, or the biggest, chewiest, yummiest cookies ever—Chocolate Chip, Peanut Butter, or Peanut Butter Chocolate Chip.

Best of all is the warm, comfortable atmosphere. You'll go home with a smile on your face—and a couple of cookies to munch on the way.

The Engine House Deli, #9 Lexington Avenue (US 60), Winchester, is just a few steps from Main Street. It is open 8 a.m. to 10 p.m., Monday through Saturday, with continuous service. (606)744-0560. Dress is casual, beer is available, reservations are not necessary, and charge cards are not accepted; personal checks accepted. ($)

ENGINE HOUSE DRESSING

1 cup oil
1/4 cup vinegar
1/4 cup lemon juice
1 teaspoon salt

1 teaspoon sugar
1 teaspoon
  Italian seasoning
1/2 teaspoon onion salt

In screw-top jar, combine ingredients and shake well.
Serves 6.

ENGINE HOUSE
SUGAR-FREE CORN BREAD WAFFLES

1 egg
2 Tablespoons butter,
  melted
2 cups yellow corn meal

1 teaspoon baking soda
1 teaspoon salt
2 cups buttermilk

In bowl, lightly beat egg and add melted butter; stir in dry
ingredients and then buttermilk. Ladle onto hot waffle iron
and cook according to manufacturer's directions. "Makes a
bunch."

ENGINE HOUSE BROWNIES

8 ounces shortening
2 cups sugar
4 eggs
1 1/2 teaspoons almond
  extract

1/3 cup sifted cocoa
2 cups sifted flour
1 cup chocolate chips
1 cup crushed pecans

In bowl, cream shortening with sugar; add eggs and flavoring.
Mix cocoa with flour and add to mixture; stir in chips and
nuts and blend well. Pour into greased 9"x 13" pan and bake
at 325 degrees 25 minutes. Cut while warm. Yields 24.

DUNCAN TAVERN
Paris

$\mathbf{W}$hen Major Joseph Duncan built his imposing stone tavern in 1788, he had an eye to the future: his elegant 3-story building contained 20 rooms, although surrounding buildings, including the Bourbon County Courthouse, were simple log structures. A ballroom, billiard room, and basement barroom are mentioned in early writing, and handsome original woodwork, blue ash floors, doors and their intricate locks remain as examples of the fine craftsmanship employed. Among early visitors were Daniel Boone, Simon Kenton, Colonel James Smith, and Governor James Garrard.

Left a young widow with six children, Anne Duncan built an adjacent house about 1803 in which to live, and leased the tavern, which operated for over 150 years under various names. In 1940, Duncan Tavern was deeded to the Kentucky Society, Daughters of the American Revolution, who restored and furnished it as their state shrine. The Anne Duncan House was acquired in 1955, and its restoration incorporated fine cabinetwork from many historic Kentucky buildings which had been demolished.

The two buildings, placed on the National Register in 1973, are open to the public for tours. On view are mementos of famous early Kentuckians and a collection of fine antique Kentucky furniture donated by D.A.R. members and friends. In the former tavern basement, The John Fox, Jr. Library, dedicated to the beloved Kentucky author of *The Little Shepherd of Kingdom Come*, houses a historical and genealogical library which is available for use.

Meals are no longer served on a regular basis at Duncan Tavern, but it is a famous catering center, and groups of 20 or more may schedule meals, receptions, or parties by appointment. Called "a gracious old place to have a party," Duncan Tavern is known for its carefully prepared, attractively served food. Parties may be scheduled for brunch, coffee, luncheon, tea, and dinner, weddings, and receptions.

Food chosen for a reception might be spiced tea, finger sandwiches, pecan tassies and petit fours, plus dips with fresh vegetables, little quiches, fresh fruit dipped in chocolate, and puff paste filled with chicken salad. Luncheon or dinner entrées of chicken, ham, or prime rib are accompanied by vegetable casseroles, corn soufflé, yeast rolls or strawberry bread, and topped off with something delicious.

Duncan Tavern, 323 High Street, Paris, is open for tours Tuesday through Saturday, from 10 a.m. to 12 noon, and from 1 to 4 p.m., and on Sunday from 1:30 to 4 p.m. The library is open during the same hours. (606)987-1788. Meals are served only to groups of 20 or more by prior arrangement, usually several months in advance, and price is determined by the menu. No charge cards; personal checks accepted. Tour cost is $1.50 for adults, $.80 for children; library use is $2.00 a day.

DUNCAN TAVERN CHEESE PUDDING*

10 slices white bread, trimmed and cubed
4 ounces butter or margarine, melted
1 pound grated sharp cheese

3 eggs separated
2 cups milk
1/2 teaspoon salt
1/4 teaspoon red pepper
1/2 teaspoon dry mustard

In large bowl, toss bread cubes in melted butter; alternate layers of bread cubes and grated cheese in well-greased casserole. Beat egg yolks and mix with remaining ingredients; pour over cheese and bread cubes. Beat egg whites stiff but not dry; fold into mixture. Let stand overnight in refrigerator. Bake at 325 degrees 45 to 50 minutes or until firm. Serves 8.

DUNCAN TAVERN POTATO YEAST ROLLS*

1 cup mashed, boiled potatoes,
1 cup potato water, lukewarm
1 package yeast

1/2 cup sugar
1 teaspoon salt
3 cups flour
1/3 cup vegetable oil

In saucepan, cook potatoes until tender; drain, reserving 1 cup cooking water, mash, and measure. Dissolve yeast in lukewarm potato water; add sugar, salt, and potatoes. Add flour a little at a time; add oil. Cover with waxed paper and place in refrigerator. Make up rolls as needed, allow to rise in warm place until doubled, and bake at 400 degrees.

DUNCAN TAVERN
ORANGE ICE BOX COOKIES*

1 cup shortening
  or margarine
1/2 cup (packed) brown
  sugar
1/2 cup sugar
1/4 teaspoon baking soda
  IN 2 Tablespoons
  orange juice

1 Tablespoon
  grated orange rind
1 egg, lightly beaten
1/4 teaspoon salt
2 3/4 cups flour
Chopped pecans

Combine all ingredients; form into roll and let stand in refrigerator overnight. Slice and bake on ungreased cookie sheet at 350 degrees about 10 minutes.

DUNCAN TAVERN PECAN MACAROONS*

Pinch of salt
1 cup ground pecans

1 cup (packed) brown
  sugar
1 egg white, beaten stiff

Sprinkle salt over nuts; stir into sugar, and moisten mixture with egg white. Drop (or roll into small balls) on buttered cookie sheet and bake at 310 degrees 15 minutes or until light tan. Let cool 10 or 15 minutes before removing with spatula.

BOONE TAVERN
Berea

Berea college, in the quaint little community "where the Bluegrass meets the mountains," began in 1855 as a tiny non-sectarian and interracial school for needy Appalachian children. Today, 1500 students, 80 per cent of them from the Southern Appalachians, benefit from Berea's unique work-study program.

Every student works at least 10 hours a week while carrying a full academic load, defraying all or part of board, room, and health fees. Tuition is guaranteed, supported by endowment and gifts. Berea Student Industries is a source of income for the college, and the high-quality student crafts are available in college shops and through catalog sales.

In addition to working in woodcraft, wrought iron, weaving, lapidary, needlecraft, broomcraft and ceramics, students provide service in the college stores, farms, and laundry. About 150 of them, many studying hotel management, work in the Boone Tavern Hotel and Dining Room. They wait tables, man the reception desk, work as bellhops and bookkeepers, and apprentice in the kitchen. Their eager-to-please service and bright young faces have helped to attract an ever-growing clientele, many of whom return year after year.

Boone Tavern was opened in 1909 as a 25-room guest house for the college, and rapidly became a popular stopover. Expanded in 1928, the three-story Georgian-style building covers most of a city block; antique reproduction furniture throughout the hotel is from Student Industries. The dining room has many-paned windows overlooking the campus, and the overall atmosphere is one of homelike comfort.

Richard T. Hougen, Manager of Boone Tavern from 1940 to 1976, established and was head of the Hotel Management Department at Berea College. During his tenure he wrote three cookbooks which formed the basis for Boone Tavern's updated Southern cuisine. His recipes are still used, and the books are available in the lobby.

Fresh regional foods, often purchased from local farmers, are cleverly seasoned and attractively presented. Mountain brook trout, lamb, chicken, beef, and roast turkey are typical selections, and each meal comes with appetizer, salad, entrée, fresh vegetables and dessert, plus relishes at dinner. Two wonderful hot breads are passed at each meal (the spoonbread, served only at dinner, is legendary). For dessert, top off a satisfying experience with Saigon Chocolate Pie (cinnamon crumb crust!) Cherry Crisp, Pecan Pie, or Old South Peach Pie with ice cream.

Boone Tavern, Berea, is open 7 days a week. Breakfast is 7 to 9 a.m.; lunch, Monday through Saturday, is 11:30 a.m. to 1:30 p.m.; Sunday 12 noon to 2 p.m.; dinner is 6 to 7:30 p.m. (606)986-9358. Berea is 40 miles south of Lexington, just east of I-75. Jackets, required for men, will be provided for those without. Reservations are requested; they are important during Craftsmen's Fairs the second weekend of May, July, and October. There is a strict no-tipping policy, and there are 57 overnight rooms. AE,DC,DS,MC,V. ($$)

BOONE TAVERN SOUTHERN SPOON BREAD*

3 cups milk
1 1/2 cups
    white corn meal
3 eggs, beaten
1 teaspoon salt

1 3/4 teaspoons
    baking powder
2 Tablespoons
    melted butter

In large pan, bring milk to boil; stir in corn meal, stirring constantly to prevent scorching. Cook until thick, remove from heat, and allow to cool; mixture will be very stiff. Using mixer, beat in remaining ingredients and beat 15 minutes. Pour into well-greased casserole and bake at 375 degrees 30 minutes.

BOONE TAVERN
CREAM OF PIMIENTO SOUP*

2 Tablespoons butter
3 Tablespoons flour
1/2 teaspoon salt
Dash pepper

1/2 teaspoon grated onion
3 cups milk
4 cups chicken stock
1/2 cup pimientos, sieved

In pan, melt butter; stir in flour and seasonings and blend well. Add milk, stock, and pimientos and simmer 20 to 30 minutes, stirring constantly until thickened. Serves 10.

BOONE TAVERN
PORK CHOPS SOME TRICKY WAY*

4 lean pork chops
1/2 cup tomato paste
1/2 cup grated
  Parmesan cheese

1 cup bread crumbs
Oil for sautéeing
Sauce (below)

Trim chops and brush to coat with tomato paste. Mix cheese and bread crumbs and pat onto chops. In skillet, brown chops on both sides. Transfer chops to casserole and add a small amount of water to prevent sticking. Bake at 350 degrees 1 hour. Serve with sauce. Serves 4.

For sauce: thicken 2 cups chicken stock with a paste of 2 1/2 Tablespoons flour and a little stock. Cook 5 minutes. Add 3/4 cup sliced mushrooms.

BOONE TAVERN
CHICKEN FLAKES IN BIRDS NEST*

4 medium
  Idaho potatoes,
  coarsely grated
Deep fat for frying

5 cups chicken
  cream sauce (below)
4 cups cooked chicken,
  diced

Thinly line a 4-inch strainer with grated potatoes. Place a 2-inch strainer inside larger strainer to hold potatoes in place. Fry until golden brown; remove nest (tap or ease with knife) and allow to cool; reheat in oven before serving. Place nest on plate and fill with chicken/sauce mixture. Serves 8.

For sauce: blend 1 cup chicken fat with 1 cup flour and cook 5 minutes. Stir in 6 cups hot chicken stock; cook 10 minutes to thicken. Ladle 5 cups into another pan, season with salt and pepper, and stir in chicken.

*From LOOK NO FURTHER, Copyright © 1952, 1953, 1955 by Richard T. Hougen, Berea, Kentucky. Used by Permission.

THE MIKE FINK
Covington

Kentucky's northernmost and perhaps most unusual historic restaurant is a sternwheeler tow boat permanently moored on the Kentucky shore of the Ohio River, near the mouth of the Licking River. This "Point" was known to navigators before 1751, and played an important part in Kentucky's early history.

The Mike Fink had an illustrious working career—one of the last of its kind to be constructed (in 1926), it towed oil barges under the name "John W. Hubbard." In the late 1940s, as "The Charles Dorrance," its cargo changed to coal, and it pushed the longest tow of its day on the Ohio River. The vessel became a restaurant in 1968, renamed for the roistering nineteenth-century keel-boatsman whose legendary exploits made him the riverboat version of Paul Bunyan.

Placed on the National Register in 1982, The Mike Fink has a restored exterior, even to the center-cut oak paddlewheel, but the inside has been ingeniously adapted to accommodate the restaurant's enormous clientele. Former coal storage areas house the kitchens, lower-level boiler rooms now hold refrigerators and food storage, and cabins for 25 passengers have been converted to a banquet room.

The visitor, traversing a gangplank that adapts to the level of the ever-changing river, enters a spacious dining room, which recaptures the romance and elegance of the riverboat era. Velvet upholstery, glass panels etched with famous riverboats, shining brass and polished oak add to comfort and atmosphere.

One of the most noticeable features of the room is the "Raw Bar," a riverboat institution, with iced shrimp, oysters, clams, stone crab claws and Alaska king crab legs piled high, waiting to become appetizers or whole meals for seafood lovers. Another is the Captain's Galley, where certain entrées are prepared for the visual and olfactory delight of anyone at hand.

"The Barge" is permanently alongside for additional seating, and offers spectacular views of the Ohio River and the Cincinnati skyline. Its glass walls provide a 24-hour panorama of river life, whether it be a passing towboat with a string of barges, a speedboat race, a paddlewheel tour boat, or a family of ducks.

Food on The Mike Fink has a New Orleans flavor, with seafood and beef entrées predominating; giant burgers and sandwiches are added at lunch, and captains concoct such entrées as Steak Diane, Halibut Natchez, and Sautéed Seafood Supreme in the visible galley in the evening. Mississippi Bean Soup and other riverboat specialties are always on the menu, and you can finish up with creamy Key Lime Pie or Kahlua Chocolate Mousse—with a chocolate crust on top.

The Mike Fink is more than a riverboat that serves food; it is a fine restaurant that happens to be on a riverboat.

The Mike Fink, at the foot of Greenup Street, Covington, is open 7 days a week. Lunch, Monday through Saturday, is 11 a.m. to 4 p.m.; dinner, Monday through Thursday, is 4 to 10 p.m., Friday and Saturday to 11 p.m. Sunday à la carte breakfast is 10 a.m. to 2 p.m., and Sunday dinner is 2 to 10 p.m. (606)261-4212. Anchored in the Ohio River at the foot of the suspension (blue) bridge, it is about 6 blocks east of I-75. Dress is casual to dressy, all legal beverages are available, and reservations are recommended, but not required. Busiest times are during Cincinnati Reds home ball games and the Labor Day River Festival, which is pre-sold by reservation only. AE,CB,DC,MC,V. ($$$)

THE MIKE FINK SHRIMP SCAMPI

For each serving:
2 Tablespoons butter
1/2 Tablespoon
    minced fresh garlic
1/2 Tablespoon shallots
1/2 Tablespoon minced
    parsley

1/2 Tablespoon oregano
Fresh ground pepper
1 ounce white wine
6 large gulf shrimp

In small sauté pan, melt butter, add seasonings and wine; mix well. Over high heat, sauté shrimp about 1 1/2 minutes per side. Serve over rice or al denté pasta.

MIKE FINK NIÇOISE SALAD

For each serving:
Romaine lettuce, torn
Cold, cooked
  green beans
Small whole boiled
  Redskin potatoes
Pickled beets

Hard cooked egg wedges
Tomato wedges
Whole green onions
A scoop of cold tuna
Vinaigrette
  salad dressing

Toss lettuce, surround with vegetables, place tuna in center, and serve with dressing on the side.

DEE FELICE CAFÉ
Covington

During the period of western expansion, many immigrants headed down the Ohio River, and a number of them settled in the bustling little city of Covington. Chiefly of German origin, newcomers brought skills with them— there were artisans of all types, merchants, industrialists, and professionals.

In 1868, James G. Arnold, a prominent Covington builder, contracted to erect three 3-story commercial buildings. The brick structure at the northwest corner of Main and 6th Streets was to house three businesses on the street level and "a commodious hall for public meetings" above.

Edward L. Pieck, a Covington native of German extraction and a graduate pharmacist, moved into the corner store in 1885. Other tenants were a confectioner and a barber downstairs, and the I.O.O.F. (Odd Fellows) Hall on the third floor.

By 1890, Pieck had expanded into the center store, opening the wall between and supporting the span with slender columns. Pictures at that time show hand-carved cherry cabinets, a molded tin ceiling, and a marble floor, with a cast iron store-front. Few changes have been made, although two elegant rooms, with stained glass windows, a tented ceiling, and magnificent oak mantels, were added at the rear around the turn of the century as part of the owner's residence.

The building remained a pharmacy until 1971, when it became an antiques shop. As part of the West Side/Main Strasse Historic District, it was placed on the National Register in 1983.

Dee Felice, a popular Cincinnati jazz musician and band leader who has traveled and performed with Mel Torme, Julius La Rosa, James Brown, and Sergio Mendez, had searched for a place in which to open a jazz club and restaurant. The corner store was perfect, and the café opened in March of 1984, its Victorian refinements virtually unspoiled.

The embossed tin ceiling was picked out in gold leaf, and the wide molded tin cornice and frieze were enhanced with paint in gray and unusual shades of pink. Back rooms are now intimate dining rooms, and the third store has been included, with arches into the main room where Felice holds forth on a stage behind the bar, playing jazz with his Sleepcat Dixieland Band on weekends. On other nights, except Mondays, there are trios or piano players—always jazz, and always lively.

The Dee Felice Café was immediately popular; operated by family and long-time employees, it is a friendly, upbeat place where great music and superb food vie for your attention. Fiery New Orleans entrées (just right with jazz) include succulent Jambalaya and Blackened 12-ounce Strip Steaks; homemade pastas have creative sauces (shrimp and artichoke hearts in lobster butter, for example); and chef's specialties such as Salmon Antonetta (baked, with a sour cream/yogurt/dill sauce) and Chicken Martinelli (boneless breast, braised with oysters, herb butter, and sparkling apple cider) round out a varied menu.

Among desserts are Opera Crème Torte, Apple Bavarian Cheesecake, Carrot Cake, and the house specialty, Boule de Neige, a rich, dense mound of chocolate, frosted with whipped cream.

Dee Felice Café, 529 Main Street, Covington, is open 7 days a week. Lunch, Monday through Friday, is 11 a.m. to 2:30 p.m.; dinner begins at 5 p.m., served Sunday through Tuesday until 10 p.m., Wednesday and Thursday until 11 p.m., and Friday and Saturday until 12 midnight. (606)261-2365. There is live entertainment Tuesday through Sunday nights. Dress is "dressy casual," all legal beverages are available, and reservations are strongly suggested on weekends; tables booked before 9 p.m. are limited to 2 hour occupancy. AE,DC,MC,V. ($$)

DEE FELICE CAFÉ CHICKEN PICCATA

3 small whole chicken breasts, split, skinned, and boned	2 teaspoons butter
	1 small clove garlic, crushed
Flour for dusting	2 pinches parsley
1 1/2 teaspoons butter	1/2 teaspoon salt
3/4 cup white wine	1/2 teaspoon pepper
1 1/2 cups chicken stock	2 1/2 teaspoons capers

Dust chicken with flour and set aside. In skillet, melt butter and sauté breasts a few seconds, until lightly browned. Add remaining ingredients and sauté until chicken is done and sauce is slightly thickened. Serves 2.

DEE FELICE CAFÉ MIXED GREENS

3 pounds mixed greens,
 stemmed and washed
1 1/2 gallons water
2 pounds ham hocks
1 large yellow onion,
 chopped

1 1/2 Tablespoons salt
1 Tablespoon pepper
2 teaspoons Cajun spice
2 to 3 ounces
 red wine vinegar
1 Tablespoon beef base*

In large stockpot, bring all ingredients to a boil, reduce to medium heat, and let boil until tender, about 1 1/2 hours. Keeps well in refrigerator and improves with age.

*Beef base is a granulated flavoring available to restaurants; if bouillon cubes are substituted, reduce or omit salt and add salt to taste near end of cooking. Another substitution might be beef stock or bouillon as part of the liquid.

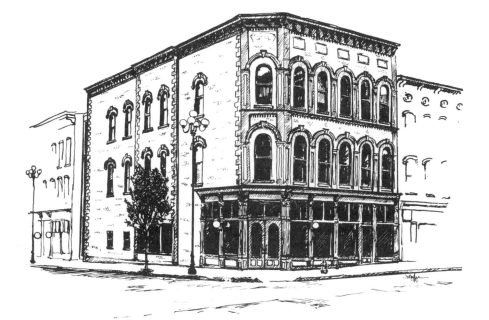

deSHĀ'S
Lexington

In June, 1775, a band of frontiersmen camped at a wilderness spring in the "Great Meadow." A pleasant spot, with ample water and good hunting, it seemed an ideal location for a settlement. As the men, including Robert Patterson and Simon Kenton, were discussing the recent first battle of the Revolution, they named the prospective town for that battle, at Lexington, Massachusetts.

It was four years before Patterson returned; with 25 men from Harrodsburg, he built a blockhouse near the middle fork of Elkhorn Creek in April of 1779. The blockhouse became one corner of a fort encircling an "unfailing" spring, lying between today's Mill Street and Broadway, south of Main Street. A town was laid out and a log courthouse constructed at the corner of Broadway (then called "Main Crossing") and Main Street. When the courthouse was relocated, the earlier building was used as the printing office of the "Kentucky Gazette," published from 1787 to 1848.

During the 1870s and '80s, a group of commercial buildings was constructed in the block bounded by Broadway, Main, Short, and Spring Streets. Incorporating such Victorian embellishments as bracketed storefronts, ornate hood moldings, and pressed tin ceilings, they housed a variety of firms. Lower floors were used as retail and manufacturing space, and owners often lived above. The Victorian Commercial Block, placed on the National Register in 1978, was adapted for use as a shopping mall in 1985.

The three-story brick structure on the corner of Main and Broadway is attributed to Phelix Lundin, a Swedish architect who is believed to have designed nine buildings on Main Street during the 1870s. Although the interior has been greatly altered, the Victorian feeling remains, with reproduction lighting fixtures and tin ceilings, oak paneling and trim, and a bar from one of Lexington's historic hostelries.

Excellent food, cozy atmosphere, and its central location made deShā's popular immediately, and it soon expanded into the adjacent building for extra dining space and the Main Cross Tavern. Hungry shoppers drop by for a snack, an appetizer, or a complete meal, chosen from a list that includes spectacular salads, homemade soups and chili, daily special entrées, and the incredible Chocolate Fudge Brownie Fix—a complete meal in itself.

deShā's, 101 North Broadway, Lexington, is open from 11 a.m. until 11 p.m. weeknights, 12 midnight weekends, and 10:30 p.m. Sundays, with continuous service. (606)259-3771. Dress is casual, all legal beverages are served, and reservations are accepted for groups of 7 or more; no reservations on weekends. AE,DC,DS,MC,V. ($$)

deSHĀ'S CORN BREAD AND HONEY BUTTER

3 cups
  self-rising cornmeal
1/3 cup sugar
6 eggs
1 1/2 cups vegetable oil

3 cups sour cream
2 2/3 cups
  cream-style corn
Honey butter

Combine ingredients in order, mixing well. Pour into greased 9" x 13" pan and bake at 350 degrees 30 minutes, or until pick comes out clean. Serve warm with honey butter.
For honey butter: mix 1 1/4 cups softened butter with 1/2 cup honey.

Note: deSha's makes this in small loaves to slice at the table—it's irresistable.

deSHĀ'S SWEET POTATO CASSEROLE

3/4 cup softened butter
1 cup sugar
4 eggs
2 1/4 teaspoons vanilla
Dash cinnamon
Dash allspice
2/3 cup heavy cream

1/2 teaspoon salt
6 cups sweet potatoes,
  cooked, peeled, and
  mashed (5 large sweet
  potatoes)
Topping

Cream butter and sugar; add remaining ingredients in order, blending well. Pour into greased 9" x 13" pan and cover with topping. Bake at 350 degrees 20 minutes. Serves 12.

For topping: melt 1 stick + 2 Tablespoons butter; stir in 1 cup brown sugar, 1/2 cup + 2 Tablespoons flour, and 1 cup chopped pecans. Mix well.

deSHĀ'S DATE NUT BREAD

2 teaspoons baking soda
2 cups boiling water
2 cups chopped dates
6 tablespoons butter
2 cups sugar

2 teaspoons vanilla
2 eggs
2 2/3 cups flour
1 cup chopped pecans

Mix soda and boiling water; pour over dates and set aside. Cream butter and sugar, beat in vanilla and eggs, then flour. Fold in date mixture and pecans. Pour into greased and floured loaf pan and bake at 350 degrees 45 to 50 minutes. Cool in pan.

deSHĀ'S LEMON ICE BOX PIE

One 9-inch
    graham cracker crust
3 eggs
Pinch salt

1 1/3 cans sweetened
    condensed milk
3/4 cup lemon juice

Beat eggs with salt, add condensed milk, then lemon juice, mixing well. Pour into crust and bake at 350 degrees 15 minutes. Chill.

DUDLEY'S RESTAURANT
Lexington

Lexington City School No. 3, known as The Dudley School, was constructed in 1881 on the site of an earlier residence which had housed the school since its creation in 1851. It was named for Dr. Benjamin Winslow Dudley, a Lexington surgeon and chairman of anatomy and surgery departments at Transylvania University Medical School.

The two-story, late-Richardsonian brick structure continued as a school until 1932. Among early instructors was Mary Desha, a founder of the Daughters of the American Revolution.

The building housed various government offices during depression and war years, but stood vacant for seven years before restoration. With the South Hill Historic District, it was placed on the National Register in 1978, and in 1980 it became Dudley Square, a unique mall of specialty shops and Dudley's Restaurant.

Available space was carefully adapted; permission was given by The Bluegrass Trust for a glass-enclosed hallway between the former principal's office and a classroom, and kitchens in "catacombs" in the basement were vented four floors to the roof. An enormous oak back bar, from a restaurant closed by prohibition, required an entire day and ten people to move; five people were needed to lift the mirror.

Today, entered from the wide hallway that echoes with the footsteps of generations of school children, Dudley's seems always to have been a restaurant. Shades of plum and green are set off by natural wood and plants; the bar is cozy and intimate, and the dining room, lighted by tall windows, is graced with linens, candles, and flowers, and serves as a gallery for local artists. In warm weather, diners linger on the patio under umbrellas and a large sycamore tree.

Food at Dudley's receives extra attention: everything is fresh and cooked to order, accommodating those on special diets. Local foods are treated in non-traditional ways, with daily appetizers, soup, fish and seafood specials, and a menu of "regulars." Appetizers and pastas are especially creative, as are rich, sweet desserts, and all entrées are served with salad or soup. Hot muffins are different each day, often combining many flavoring ingredients, and are always superb.

Dudley's Restaurant, 380 South Mill Street, Lexington, is open 7 days a week. Lunch is 11:30 a.m. to 2:30 p.m., and dinner is 5:30 to 10 p.m., until 11 p.m. Friday and Saturday. Lighter fare is available from 2:30 to 5:30 p.m. in the bar. (606)252-1010. Dress is casual, all legal beverages are served, and reservations, always a good idea, are essential on weekends. AE,MC,V. ($$)

DUDLEY'S MIXED BEAN SOUP

4 cups dried navy or great northern beans

4 cups dried black beans

Soak each variety of bean in 2 quarts water overnight. Drain, place in separate pots with 2 quarts water each, bring to boil, and add to EACH:

2 medium onions, diced fine
3 medium carrots, diced fine
4 stalks celery, diced fine

8 ozs. ham hock meat or 8 strips cooked bacon
4 cloves garlic, chopped
Chopped tomato, optional
Seasonings (below)

Lower to simmer, and cook until tender. Combine beans AFTER cooking and garnish with sour cream, chopped onion, and chopped parsley.

Season each with one of the following:
1) 3 bay leaves, 1 Tablespoon thyme, salt and pepper, Tabasco™, 1/2 teaspoon nutmeg OR
2) 1 Tablespoon turmeric, 1 teaspoon ground coriander, 1/2 teaspoon nutmeg, 1/2 teaspoon cinnamon, 1 Tablespoon cayenne OR
3) 1 Tablespoon chili powder, 2 cups salsa, 1 cup green chilies.

DUDLEY'S CHICKEN RIOJA

For each serving:
Two 3-ounce boneless chicken breasts
1 tomato, diced small

1/3 cup Greek olives, pitted and diced fine
1/2 cup bread crumbs
Salt and pepper

4 ounces country ham or
  prosciutto, diced small
1 cup ricotta or
  cottage cheese

1 egg, beaten, for coating
Bread crumbs
  for coating
Olive oil for browning

Pound chicken breasts under plastic wrap until uniform thickness; overlay 2 breasts top to bottom and pound seam to seal together. Mix tomatoes, ham, cheese, olives and bread crumbs, season, and spoon 2 ounces of mixture on breasts. Starting with two long sides of breast meat, fold one over the other and tuck in ends to close. Dip in egg, roll in bread crumbs, and brown in hot olive oil. Bake at 400 degrees until done, and serve with marinara or Parmesan sauce.

DUDLEY'S
DOUBLE LAYER CHOCOLATE GANACHE

2 cups sugar
1 3/4 cups flour
3/4 cup cocoa
1 1/2 teaspoons
  baking soda
1 1/2 teaspoons
  baking powder

1 teaspoon salt
2 eggs
1 cup milk
2 teaspoons vanilla
1/2 cup oil
1 cup hot coffee

Sift dry ingredients together. Crack eggs into milk, add vanilla, and mix well. Add oil and coffee. Add liquid ingredients to dry; mix well and divide into 2 greased and floured 9" round pans. Bake at 350 degrees 25 to 30 minutes or until toothpick inserted in center comes out clean. Fill and frost with ganache.

For ganache: In double boiler, melt 12 ounces bittersweet chocolate; remove from heat and cool to room temperature. Stir in 1 2/3 cups room temperature sour cream.

JOE BOLOGNA'S RESTAURANT
Lexington

In 1781, The Virginia General Assembly was petitioned by Lexington's Board of Trustees (Kentucky did not become a separate state until 1792) to allow the addition of 710 acres of land just south of the existing town.

Beginning at the Town Branch, or Middle Fork of The Elkhorn, which ran approximately where Vine Street does now, the new portion of Lexington was on an elevation which had long been called the "South Hill."

South Hill represents Lexington's nineteenth-century development; Federal and Greek Revival townhouses rub elbows with cottages and impressive houses of the Victorian period, and later construction of churches, a school, and commercial buildings resulted in an interesting architectural mix.

Maxwell Street, named for a prominent landowner, ran along the south boundary of South Hill. In 1890, a lot on the southeast corner of Maxwell and Upper Streets was chosen as the site of a "mission church" by Lexington's First Presbyterian Church. The existing dwelling, facing Upper Street, was used as the parsonage, and the church, constructed in a grove of maple trees and fronting on Maxwell, was dedicated in 1891.

The church was successful from the first; it achieved independence from its parent church in 1892, and outgrew its quarters in 1916, when it moved to a larger structure farther down Maxwell. The building then served as synagogue for the Ohavay Zion Congregation until it was again outgrown, in 1986. Following a sensitive adaptation, it became the new home for Joe Bologna's popular restaurant in 1989.

Despite several twentieth-century additions, the exterior of the original building is little changed, dominated by a massive stone-framed stained-glass window in the gable end. With the South Hill Historic District, it was placed on the National Register in 1978.

The interior, bathed in soft light from simple geometric stained-glass windows, presents a dramatic contrast; a loft rises in the center of the open space, creating intimate, cozy booths below, and a separate dining area above. Light woods reproduce wainscot and dividers appropriate to the building's age, and line a pleasant bar in the former chancel.

Permeated by the fragrance of the breadsticks and deep-dish pizza that have made "Joe B's" one of Lexington's favorite places, the restaurant is characterized by warm, friendly service and superb southern Italian cuisine.

Sandwiches and salads are popular at lunch, and there are lighter dishes for the health conscious—don't miss the vegetable pizza, with banana pepper rings—and, for those who have room, ice cream desserts, New York-style cheesecake, and a rich, chewy "Caramel Apple Granny."

Joe Bologna's Restaurant, 120 West Maxwell, is entered off "Maxwell's Alley" or from the rear parking lot. Additional parking is available at the corner of Maxwell and Limestone Streets. The restaurant is open 11 a.m. to 12 midnight Monday through Thursday, until 1 a.m. Friday and Saturday, and 12 noon until 11 p.m. Sunday. (606)252-4933. All legal beverages are served, dress is casual, and reservations are only accepted for parties of 10 or more, weekdays. Busiest times are U.K. football weekends, and evenings of concerts at Rupp Arena. MC,V. ($$)

JOE BOLOGNA'S
LINGUINE WITH WHITE CLAM SAUCE

4 ounces dry linguine cooked al denté	**6 1/2 ounce can clams, with liquid**
5 Tablespoons olive oil	**6 dashes pepper**
2 cloves garlic, chopped	**4 dashes oregano**
3 teaspoons parsley, chopped	

In skillet, heat olive oil and sauté garlic 2 minutes. Add parsley, sauté 1 minute, then add clam liquid and pepper and simmer 2 minutes. Add clams and oregano; simmer 2 minutes. Serve over hot, well-drained linguine. Serves 1 or 2.

JOE BOLOGNA'S FETTUCCINE ALFREDO WITH HAM, BACON, AND GREEN PEPPER

4 ounces dry fettuccine, cooked al denté
1 1/2 ounces butter (no substitute)
1 ounce green pepper, chopped
4 ounces heavy cream
2 1/2 teaspoons Parmesan cheese
Dash white pepper
1 ounce cooked ham, chopped
1/4 ounce cooked bacon, crumbled

In skillet, melt butter; when bubbling, add green pepper and simmer 3 minutes. Add cream and simmer 1 minute, then cheese and white pepper and simmer 30 seconds. Add ham and bacon and simmer 90 seconds, until thickened but not too thick. Toss with hot, well-drained fettuccine and serve. Serves 1 or 2.

JOE BOLOGNA'S FETTUCCINE AL BURRO

1 pound dry fettuccine, cooked al denté
4 ounces softened butter (no substitute)
1/4 cup heavy cream
1/2 cup grated Parmesan cheese
Salt and pepper
Freshly grated Parmesan cheese

In bowl, cream butter, beat in cream a little at a time, then gradually beat in grated cheese. Cover and set aside; if refrigerated, bring to room temperature before using. While fettuccine is cooking, heat a large serving bowl; place well-drained hot fettuccine in bowl, add butter/cheese mixture and toss thoroughly. Season. Pass extra cheese for topping. Serves 4.

THE MANSION AT GRIFFIN GATE
Lexington

When Daniel Boone and other early explorers of Kentucky returned to "The Settlements," they enthusiastically described the Bluegrass region as "The Eden of the West." Rich in trees, water, and game, the lush center of Kentucky attracted thousands.

The gentleman farmer tradition, brought from Virginia by many of her younger sons, is epitomized by comfortable country homes, a leisured way of life, and the graciousness known as "Kentucky hospitality."

Evidence of this may still be seen by the visitor who drives out the old roads that radiate from Lexington like spokes from a hub. Secluded in clumps of trees, handsome houses preside over fields of magnificent horses, surrounded by miles of stone or painted board fences.

On the Newtown Pike, near the I-64 interchange, surrounded by a golf course and new townhouses, is a house now called "The Mansion at Griffin Gate."

It was originally designed by Cincinnatus Shryock, a respected Kentucky architect, and was built in 1873 on the site of an earlier house. A two-story red brick with a cupola and a one-story porch, it was called "Highland Home," and was the boyhood home of Kentucky historian J. Winston Coleman. After the house was sold in the 1920s, the cupola and porch were removed, and the pedimented two-story porch with Ionic columns was added.

Subsequent owners changed the name to "Griffin Gate" for the winged figures at the entrance, brought in antique mantels and lighting fixtures, and attached several one-story additions. Today the house stands in grounds registered as a unique site for vegetation in Fayette County. As part of Marriott's Griffin Gate Resort, it is a fine restaurant in which Continental cuisine is presented in nine elegant, intimate dining rooms.

Lunchtime favorites include their Kentucky Hot Brown sandwich, the Almond Chicken Salad Croissant, steak sandwiches, and a huge Chef's Salad. A typical evening meal might be Scallops with Artichokes in Cream Sauce; French Onion Soup; Tournedos Helder (two petite fillets topped with lobster tail and two sauces); and Chocolate Macadamia Nut Pie. Menus change seasonally and you can look forward to some surprises, but there's always a wide variety of fresh seafood and friendly, efficient service.

The Mansion at Griffin Gate, 1720 Newtown Pike, Lexington, is open 7 days a week. Lunch, Monday through Friday, is 11:30 a.m. to 2 p.m. Dinner is 6 to 10 p.m., Monday through Thursday and Sunday, until 10:30 p.m. Friday and Saturday. (606)231-5152. Dress is casual, although most men wear coat and tie; all legal beverages are available; and reservations are recommended. AE,CB,DC,DS,JCB,MC,V. ($$$)

859

288-6142

THE MANSION SHRIMP DIJON

For each serving:
2 Tablespoons oil
5 very large
  shrimp, peeled and
  deveined

1/4 cup heavy cream
1 Tablespoon
  Dijon mustard
Chopped parsley

In sauté pan over medium heat, place oil and sauté shrimp until half-cooked. Add cream and stir. Add mustard and continue cooking until shrimp are done and sauce is creamy. Place on serving dish and garnish with parsley.

THE MANSION VEAL VERA CRUZ

1 pound boneless loin of
  veal, trimmed of all fat
1 cup flour for dredging
4 Tablespoons oil
4 Tablespoons
  white wine
1 large sweet green
  pepper, diced

1 large sweet red pepper,
  diced
1/4 cup diced
  jalapeño pepper
1/4 cup sliced black olives
2 cups shredded
  Monterey jack cheese

Cut loin across grain into 16 one-ounce portions. Place one slice on cutting board, cover with plastic wrap, and pound to 1/8" thickness. Discard plastic and repeat with all slices. Dredge veal in flour. In sauté pan, heat oil and sauté each piece 45 seconds each side; remove meat to warmed oven-proof platter. Remove sauté pan from heat and deglaze with wine; return to heat and add peppers and olives. Sauté 1 1/2 minutes, and spoon over veal. Top with cheese and place under broiler or in microwave to melt cheese. Serves 4.

THE MANSION
BREAD PUDDING AND WHISKEY SAUCE

3 cups milk
6 eggs
3/4 cup sugar
2 Tablespoons vanilla
1/4 teaspoon nutmeg
Pinch cinnamon

1/4 cup shredded coconut
1/4 cup raisins, plumped
  in boiling water
9 cups cubed bread or
  leftover Danish pastry
Whiskey sauce

Heat milk to 130 degrees. In bowl, whip eggs with sugar until thick. SLOWLY mix hot milk into eggs. Add spices, coconut, and raisins. Place cubed bread/pastry into 2-inch deep baking dish and pour custard in to just cover bread; pat bread down until evenly moistened. Bake at 300 degrees 45 to 55 minutes or until toothpick comes out clean. Serve warm, topped with whiskey sauce. Can be frozen after baking for later use.

For whiskey sauce: in double boiler, cream 8 ounces sugar with 4 ounces butter. Add 4 ounces dark brown corn syrup and 3 Tablespoons water. Cook until sugar is melted and temperature is 175 degrees. Remove from heat and gradually add 1 beaten egg, stirring vigorously. Cool to room temperature and stir in 1/4 cup bourbon whiskey. Will keep 1 week in refrigerator.

MERRICK INN
Lexington

In the Bluegrass region, famed for the excellence of its horses, none has received the acclaim of Merrick, who finished "in the money" 157 times of 203 starts. He won 64 of those races, and continued to race to a great age, running 3 times in his 12-year-old season. When he died at the age of 38 in 1941, he was the oldest of all recorded thoroughbreds.

His name lived on in the famous horse farm of J. Cal Milam, owner and trainer of other famous horses: Exterminator, Derby winner of 1918, Anna M. Humphrey, Tut Tut, Commodore, Brown Wisdom, Milkmaid, McKee, and Dust Flower.

The rolling green fields where they grazed have been submerged in suburban growth, and an apartment complex is now entered through the farm's grey stone gates, but the manor house is still known for its style and fine food.

Bordered by trim Colonial-style townhouses, the tree-lined entrance is named for Mr. Milam. Guests are cautioned to "look for a house with no signs and lots of cars"—the residential atmosphere is rigidly maintained.

Merrick Inn's welcoming entrance signals the warmth within. An eighteenth-century atmosphere prevails, with comfortable reproduction furniture, carefully chosen wallpapers, and handsome prints on the walls. Operated since the early 1970s by Bob and Libby Murray, who were joined by their son Bobby in 1989, Merrick Inn's popularity stems from food that represents the best of Regional American Cooking.

Fresh foods are simply prepared, without heavy sauces that might obscure natural flavors. Prime rib, steaks, lamb chops, and fresh salmon are always available, with three or four fresh seafood items offered as nightly specials. A host of choices such as trout (stuffed with corn bread, crab and shrimp), wall-eye pike, chicken breasts sautéed with Bing cherries, and roast pork loin (with applesauce and dressing) reflect the seasons. Vegetables are fresh and often ingeniously prepared, and hot rolls, muffins and desserts are all homemade.

Served at fireside on brisk winter nights, Merrick Place food has a comforting quality, but lighter summer fare and salads are equally desirable on the patio, where guests like to linger on warm summer nights.

859 area code

Merrick Inn, 3380 Tate's Creek Road, Lexington, is open for dinner only, Monday through Thursday from 5:30 to 10, until 10:30 Friday and Saturday. (606)269-5417. Merrick Place is just inside the New Circle Road (Circle 4), east of Tate's Creek Pike, across from The Lansdowne Shoppes; follow Milam Lane to Merrick Inn. Coats are preferred for men indoors; patio dress is "casual in good taste." All legal beverages are available, and reservations are almost a necessity, particularly when football weekends coincide with Keeneland. AE,DC,MC,V ($$)

MERRICK INN FISH FILLETS WELLINGTON

**Two 1/2-pound fillets
(whitefish, grouper
sole)
1 Tablespoon lemon juice
1/4 teaspoon salt
1/4 teaspoon pepper**

**1 can refrigerated
crescent rolls or frozen
pastry dough
Crab stuffing
Yolk of 1 egg, mixed
with a little water**

Season fillets and set aside. Separate dough into 2 portions; on floured board, roll out 1 portion and cut into fish shape; cut a second fish shape 1" larger all around. Place smaller shape on greased baking sheet and spread with stuffing. Top with fillet, half the remaining stuffing, then repeat, and cover with larger shape, pinching edges to seal. With scrap dough, cut out eyes, fins, and gills. Brush with egg mixture and bake 10 minutes at 425 degrees, then 15 minutes at 350 degrees, until crust is brown and fillets are opaque and flake when tested. Serves 4.

For stuffing: combine 1/2 pound flaked crab meat, 1 egg white, 1/3 cup lowfat yogurt, 1/2 cup chopped celery, 1 Tablespoon chopped onion, 1/2 cup bread crumbs, 1/4 cup melted butter, and 1 teaspoon lemon pepper.

MERRICK INN
TOMATO BISQUE WITH CROUTONS

6 Tablespoons
   unsalted butter
2 large ripe tomatoes,
   chopped
1 carrot, peeled and
   chopped
1 celery stalk, chopped
1 small onion, chopped
1 clove garlic, crushed
28-ounce can
   crushed tomatoes
3/4 cup tomato juice
3 Tablespoons
   tomato paste
2 Tablespoons
   brown sugar

1/4 teaspoon
   white pepper
1/2 pound mushrooms,
   sliced
1 1/2 teaspoons
   fresh chopped parsley
1/2 teaspoon
   fresh oregano or
   pinch of dried
1/2 teaspoon fresh basil
   or pinch of dried
1/2 teaspoon fresh thyme
   or pinch of dried
1 cup heavy cream
2 cups chicken stock or
   canned broth

In large heavy pot, melt 2 Tablespoons butter. Add half of the chopped vegetables and cook 10 minutes, stirring occasionally. Add garlic and cook 2 minutes. Mix in next 5 ingredients, cover and simmer 1 1/2 hours, stirring occasionally. Cool mixture and purée in batches in blender. Set aside. In large heavy pan, melt remaining butter and add remaining chopped vegetables with mushrooms and herbs. Sauté until tender, about 8 minutes, then stir in puréed mixture and cream; soup will be very thick. Add enough stock to thin to desired consistency. Heat through, stirring frequently, and serve. Can be prepared one day ahead to this point, covered and refrigerated.

For croutons: toss 2 cups cubed French bread with 1/4 cup melted butter and grated Parmesan cheese. Bake at 350 degrees until brown, tossing occasionally.

THE MAIN STREET HOUSE
Nicholasville

According to legend, Jessamine Douglass, the young daughter of an early settler, was sitting on the creekbank near her cabin home when she was tomahawked by an Indian. The creek was named for her, and the county, taken from Fayette in 1798, was named for the creek. It is the only county in Kentucky named, even indirectly, for a woman.

Among the brave and interesting people who opened up Kentucky to settlement was Major Benjamin Netherland, born in Powhattan County, Virginia, in 1755. Known as "hero of the Battle of Blue Licks," he built a cabin that year, 1782, in what is now Nicholasville, to which he returned in 1793. The inn he established, Mingo Tavern, also served as post office; he was postmaster for 20 years. When the Jessamine County seat was laid out around the intersection of several trails, his became the first residence in town.

Early county courts were probably held at Mingo Tavern; Jessamine County's first real courthouse was a small red brick building constructed in 1823. Described as "uncomfortable and inconvenient," it was replaced by the present structure in 1878, during a period when much of downtown Nicholasville was under construction.

A few blocks south of the courthouse, diagonally across from the site of Mingo Tavern, a cross-gabled Queen Anne-style frame house was built about 1897. With its cutaway bay windows, inset porch, and steep gables, it has both charm and distinction, and has served as a boarding house for young women attending school, an antiques store, and a nursery school.

The house was bought by the Gibson family in 1989, and opened as a restaurant in 1990. Beautifully decorated, with fresh paint and wallpaper—and pocket doors discovered during renovation—The Main Street House has become a popular dining spot for local residents and visitors who enjoy Nicholasville's many antiques shops.

Traditional American Cuisine seems just right for this old house: homey, substantial, and evocative of simpler times. That's what you can expect, with a few surprises. Although the menu is not "health conscious," there's a delicious plate of steamed seasonal vegetables, a variety of salads, and grilled and broiled meats that will leave room for the rich desserts.

Lunchtime sandwiches include chicken or seafood

salad on croissants, Classic Club, and Boneless Pork Chop (spiced, grilled, on a bun). Homemade soups (Chicken Noodle is particularly good) vary daily, and there's a nice choice of hot entrées; the Kentucky Hot Brown is the most popular, year round.

At dinner, a juicy two-inch-thick pork chop is the house specialty; pastas have interesting sauces (Kentucky style has country ham and garlic in cream); and House Chicken is chargrilled with lemon pepper. Entrées come with plenty of side choices, plus fat puffy yeast rolls with strawberry butter.

There are always cheesecakes for dessert—Grand Marnier, peanut butter-chocolate chip, blackberry—and great pies. The Main Street Pie is full of butterscotch, coconut, and walnuts. Don't miss it.

The Main Street House, 223 South Main Street, Nicholasville, is at the corner of Broadway, and is open for lunch, Monday through Saturday, 11 a.m. to 3 p.m.; for dinner, 5 to 9 p.m., Monday through Thursday; until 10 p.m. Friday and Saturday. (606)887-1405. Dress is casual, reservations are accepted, and busiest times include the Jessamine Jamboree in early October and those Sundays (Easter, Mothers' Day, etc.) when the restaurant is open. AE,MC,V, personal checks. ($$)

THE MAIN STREET HOUSE
COCONUT FRIED SHRIMP

2 pounds large shrimp   **1/2 teaspoon salt**
2 cups flour, divided   **2 cups shredded coconut**
1 1/2 cups milk   **Vegetable oil for frying**

Peel and devein shrimp. Measure 1/2 cup flour into shallow pan; set aside. In bowl, combine remaining flour with milk and salt. Place coconut in shallow pan. Dredge shrimp in flour, then batter, then roll in coconut. Fry in 350 degree oil until coconut is golden brown; drain on absorbent paper. Serve hot with sweet-and-sour sauce. Serves 6.

MAIN STREET HOUSE SHRIMP SCAMPI

2 pounds medium
  shrimp
1/4 cup
  chopped green onion
1/4 cup chopped parsley
4 cloves garlic, crushed
3/4 cup butter or
  margarine, melted

1/4 cup dry white wine
2 Tablespoons
  lemon juice
3/4 teaspoon salt
1/4 teaspoon
  fresh pepper

Peel and devein shrimp. In skillet, sauté onion, parsley, and garlic in butter until onion is tender. Reduce heat to low; add shrimp and cook, stirring frequently, 3 to 5 minutes. With slotted spoon, remove shrimp to serving dish and keep warm. Add remaining ingredients to pan and simmer 2 minutes. Pour over shrimp. Serves 4.

MAIN STREET HOUSE
BUTTERMILK COCONUT PIE

Two 9-inch
  unbaked pie shells
2 cups sugar
1/2 cup melted butter

5 eggs, beaten
1 teaspoon vanilla
1 cup buttermilk
1 cup shredded coconut

Mix sugar with remaining ingredients in order given. Pour into pie shells and bake at 325 degrees 1 hour or until golden brown.

MAIN STREET HOUSE PEANUT BUTTER PIE

One 9-inch
  graham cracker crust
1 cup powdered sugar
1/2 cup milk

1 cup peanut butter
8 ounces cream cheese
9 ounces
  whipped topping

Mix sugar with remaining ingredients and pour into crust. Chill.

ACADEMY INN
Lancaster

Pioneers were always on the move, and trails in the wilderness were important connections between outposts. The road from Boonesboro, Daniel Boone's first fort, to Harrodsburg, the first permanent settlement in Kentucky, was heavily traveled. Where it intersected with the Lexington-Crab Orchard route, a band of Pennsylvanians established a little crossroads community in 1798. They called it "Lancaster," for their former home in Pennsylvania.

That same year, the Kentucky Legislature granted a charter to The Lancaster Male Academy, with a state grant of 5600 acres of rich land in Pulaski County to maintain it. The original school, built by the Masons about 1806, had a meeting room for their use on the second floor. It was destroyed by fire with all the Academy records, so little is known about the character of the school, or its early years. The land, however, was sold bit by bit to pay school expenses.

The present building, a simple one-story Victorian cottage, was built on the site about 1875. It remained a school for only ten years, but evidence of schoolboy occupation may still be seen; boys with knives must leave their marks—and often their names—for posterity.

After the school closed, the little building served as a residence and boarding house, owned by the same individual from 1913 until 1980. It was opened as a restaurant in 1983, and was placed on the National Register in 1984.

Students would have enjoyed the home-like atmosphere that characterizes The Academy Inn today. Painted a cheerful yellow, the deceptively small brick building still wears a residential air, and sits in a quiet lawn just a block from US 27.

Three dining rooms and a large hall are attractively decorated in shades of deep rose, dark green, and cream. In two cozy parlor-like rooms, tables cluster around fireplaces; larger tables in the big room are gauged to seat family groups or organizations for the many parties and meetings held at the Inn.

Academy Inn has become known for Southern hospitality and good food—and plenty of it. You can expect delicious oven-fried chicken on the weekday buffet, which frequently features mashed potatoes, green beans, and the Inn's famous corn pudding, varied by other vegetables, or one of the sweet potato specialties. At every meal, yeasty hot homemade rolls are fragrant and yummy. In summer, there are sandwiches and salads; winter offerings are hearty.

Sundays and evenings, chicken is joined by another meat—perhaps popular stuffed peppers, liver and onions, meatloaf, or beef Stroganoff. Friday is Catfish Night, with fried potatoes, baked beans, fresh coleslaw, and macaroni and cheese. For dessert, consider chocolate, coconut, or butterscotch pie—the latter a real, nostalgic treat—seasonal cheesecakes, or creamy Frozen Banana Salad.

The Academy Inn, 108 South Campbell Street, Lancaster, is on the corner of Buford. It is open 11:30 a.m. to 2 p.m. Sunday through Friday for lunch. Dinner is 5:30 to 8:30 p.m. Tuesday AND Friday; winter hours to 7:30 p.m. (606)792-3812. Lancaster is about 30 miles south of Lexington via US 27. Dress is casual, although most men wear coat and tie Sunday noon. Reservations are always accepted and are required on Sundays; no charge cards are accepted; personal checks accepted. ($)

ACADEMY INN FROZEN BANANA SALAD

16 ounces sour cream
20 ounces crushed
   pineapple
3 bananas,
   peeled and chopped

1/2 cup chopped walnuts
Chopped
   maraschino cherries
3 teaspoons salt

In large bowl, mix all ingredients. Pour into container sprayed with vegetable oil spray and freeze overnight. May be served as salad or dessert.

ACADEMY INN SWEET POTATO SOUFFLÉ

3 cups	1/3 cup flour
cooked sweet potatoes	1/2 cup milk
4 Tablespoons	1/2 teaspoon salt
margarine, melted	1/2 teaspoon nutmeg
2 eggs	1 teaspoon vanilla

In large bowl of mixer, whip all ingredients together; pour into baking dish sprayed with vegetable oil spray. Bake at 325 degrees 35 to 40 minutes. Remove from oven, sprinkle with topping, and bake another 5 minutes.

For topping: mix 1/2 cup brown sugar, 4 Tablespoons margarine, 1/2 cup chopped walnuts, and 1/3 cup flour until crumbly.

ACADEMY INN
SAM BOURNE'S PUMPKIN CHEESE ROLL

3 eggs	1 teaspoon soda
1 cup sugar	3/4 cup flour
1 teaspoon lemon juice	2/3 cup cooked pumpkin
1 teaspoon ginger	1 cup chopped nuts
1/2 teaspoon nutmeg	Powdered sugar
1/4 teaspoon salt	Cheese filling

In large bowl of mixer, beat eggs on high speed 1 minute. Gradually add next 6 ingredients; fold in flour and pumpkin. Spread in greased and floured cookie sheet and sprinkle with nuts. Bake at 375 degrees 20 minutes. Cool a few minutes; turn onto smooth towel that has been sprinkled with powdered sugar. Roll up, towel and all, and let stand. After making filling, unroll cake, spread with filling, and re-roll. Wrap in foil and store in refrigerator. Slice and serve.

For filling: Beat together until smooth: 1 cup confectioners sugar, 1 teaspoon vanilla, 4 Tablespoons softened butter, and 8 ounces cream cheese.

HOLLY HILL INN
Midway

Some of the most beautiful horse country in the world may be found in Woodford County, Kentucky—black or white plank fences and hand stacked gray stone walls border lush green fields where horses graze contentedly, and spacious Colonial homes are glimpsed through sheltering trees. This area typifies what many people think of when they hear the word "Kentucky."

Shady lanes through the gently rolling countryside lead to the little railroad village of Midway. Called "the first town in Kentucky built by a railroad," Midway has changed little since 1832; it still has tracks down the middle of its main street, now lined with specialty shops in historic buildings. Comfortable Victorian-era houses surround the "downtown," and the entire town was placed on the National Register of Historic Places in 1978.

The house that was to become Holly Hill Inn was built about 1850, on the site of an early stagecoach inn that burned. Enlarged and remodeled in the late 1890s, when the graceful bowed Classical Revival porch was added, it was made an inn in 1979 by Rex and Rose Lyons, who preserve a pleasant atmosphere in this quiet country setting, just a short drive from Lexington.

Some of the antiques are original to the house, including an elaborate overmantel in the library, similar to one in Charles Dickens' house in England; a handsome Kentucky walnut corner cupboard in the main dining room; and a half-canopy bed in one of the guest rooms. Additional antiques, old brass, the Greek Revival cherry woodwork, and restrained decorating in a scheme of Empire green contribute to the perfect setting for "Typical Kentucky Dining."

Holly Hill's menu changes frequently, but favorite offerings recur in the cozy dining rooms. Among these are Chicken Kiev, Marinated Beef Tenderloin, Baked Country Ham, and Broiled Lemon-Pepper Shrimp. All are served with one of the Inn's unusual soups, salad, beautifully prepared vegetables, and homemade hot breads.

At lunch, you might find Chicken Salad in a Tomato, with fresh fruit; a three-salad plate with chicken, pasta, and fruit salads, or the popular Hot Brown Sandwich. Desserts include French Silk Pie, English Trifle with Fresh Strawberries, and a selection of homemade cheesecakes.

Holly Hill Inn, North Winter Street, Midway, is open Tuesday through Saturday. Lunch is 11:30 a.m. to 2:30 p.m.; dinner is 5:30 to 9 p.m. (606)846-4732. Midway is 12 miles west of Lexington via I-64 or US 421. Dress is informal, and wine is available. Reservations are strongly recommended, especially during Keeneland season, April and October. There are 3 overnight rooms. MC,V. ($$)

HOLLY HILL INN PINK STRAWBERRY SOUP*

4 cups fresh strawberries, sliced and crushed	**1/4 cup sugar**
	Pinch salt
	3 Tablespoons arrowroot
3 cups port wine	**1/4 cup water**
2 cups orange juice	**1/2 cup heavy cream**

In non-reactive pan, mix first three ingredients and bring to boil. Stir in sugar and salt; mix arrowroot with water until smooth and blend in. Cook gently until thickened. Chill. Serve in bowls swirled with cream.

HOLLY HILL INN CHEESE ROLLS*

1 package dry yeast	**2 1/2 cups flour**
1/4 cup warm water	**2 Tablespoons chopped green pepper**
1/3 cup milk	
1/2 cup softened butter	**1 Tablespoon chopped pimiento**
1 egg	
2 Tablespoons sugar	**1/3 cup finely grated cheddar cheese**
1/2 teaspoon salt	

Dissolve yeast in warm water. In large bowl of mixer, combine next 5 ingredients at low speed; add 1 1/2 cups flour. Mix in dissolved yeast and beat 1 minute at medium; add vegetables and remaining flour. Stir in cheese and spoon into greased muffin cups. Cover and let rise 1 hour. Bake at 400 degrees 20 minutes, or until golden brown.

Note: Rose sometimes adds 3 Tablespoons crumbled crisp bacon with cheese.

HOLLY HILL INN SAUSAGE APPLE RING*

1 pound hot pork sausage	2 eggs, slightly beaten 1/2 cup milk
1 pound mild pork sausage	1/2 cup grated carrot 1/2 cup chopped
1 1/2 cups dry bread crumbs	green onion, with tops 1 cup chopped apple

Combine first 8 ingredients well. Press lightly into greased ring mold; turn out into shallow baking dish. Bake at 350 degrees 1 hour, or until done. Fill center with eggs scrambled with cheese. Sprinkle with parsley.

Note: this brunch dish may be varied with sliced mushrooms, red or green pepper, etc., added to eggs.

HOLLY HILL BUTTERMILK POUND CAKE
WITH LEMON GLAZE*

1 cup butter	2 Tablespoons vanilla
2 cups sugar	2 Tablespoons
4 eggs	lemon extract
1/4 teaspoon baking soda	1 teaspoon
1 cup buttermilk	almond extract
3 cups flour	Lemon Glaze
1/4 teaspoon salt	

In large bowl, cream butter with sugar until fluffy. Add eggs one at a time, beating well. Dissolve soda in buttermilk; combine flour and salt and add to creamed mixture, alternating with buttermilk and mixing well. Stir in flavorings. Pour into greased and floured 10" tube pan. Bake at 350 degrees 1 hour and 15 minutes, or until tests done. Cool 10 minutes, remove from pan, and spoon Lemon Glaze over cake.

For Lemon Glaze: mix 1 cup powdered sugar, 1/4 cup melted butter, and 1/3 cup lemon juice.

UPTOWN CHATTER
Versailles

W hen Kentucky became a state in 1792, Woodford county was one of its nine counties, having been formed in 1788 from part of Fayette County. It was named for General William Woodford, a Revolutionary officer of Virginia, and its county seat, Versailles (pronounced Ver-SALES), was named for the palace of the kings of France, in recognition of aid given to Americans by Louis XVI during the Revolutionary War.

As the trading center of an agricultural county rich in soil and comfortable in population, Versailles grew rapidly, reaching a population of nearly 1500 by 1870. Much of its commercial area, surrounding the Courthouse on three sides, was destroyed by fires in the 1880s and in 1896; the present downtown, rebuilt during a few years, still retains its nineteenth century character, and a recent Main Street Program has aided in refurbishing and restoring many commercial buildings to their original appearance.

Across from the Courthouse, a quaint two-story building with a bracketed cornice, diapered stonework, and the only remaining ornamental cupola in Versailles, was built in the 1880s on the site of a building lost to fire. Believed to have been a grocery during its entire existence, it changed hands only three or four times in 100 years. In its last use as a grocery, it served for more than 40 years as the C & D Market, known for quality meats and delivery service. Outlines of food pictures painted on the front still remain, etched deep into the glass.

Tim and Judy Johnson bought the market in 1988 and reclaimed the badly deteriorated structure over the years, with new roof, wiring, and plumbing. The second floor had never been finished; used to store country hams that had dripped on the floor for years, it required total renovation for its present use as office space and a small bed and breakfast operation.

The first floor, clean, bright and decorated in mauve and black, is a delightful restaurant that retains only the handsome tin ceiling as a reminder of its grocery days.

Uptown Chatter, opened in 1990 by Jayne Furnish and Sharron Klein, provides a soup/salad/sandwich menu with a difference. Typical homemade soups might be cheesy broccoli, country bean, or cabbage caraway; salads include summer seafood with curry mayonnaise and spinach salad with mandarin oranges and hot poppyseed dressing; and sandwiches might be filled with homemade pimiento cheese, olive nut, or country ham salad. Freshly homemade muffins accompany many dishes: among favorites are lemon poppyseed, banana nut, and orange cranberry.

Dining by candlelight is new to Versailles, and here, too, are differences. The atmosphere is romantic, but food is hearty and flavorful. One entrée is offered each evening (plus the regular menu) with vegetable, starch, rolls, and a choice of salad for a generous meal. You might find oven Swiss steak, beef tenderloin, stuffed cabbage rolls, or prime rib; you'll be glad you did, even if you have no room left for cheesecake, wonderful homemade pies and cobblers, and bread pudding that is a meal in itself.

Uptown Chatter, 160 South Main Street, Versailles, is open 6 days a week. Monday through Thursday, hours are 11 a.m. to 8 p.m.; Friday and Saturday to 10 p.m., with continuous service. Versailles is 12 miles west of Lexington, 14 miles southeast of Frankfort. (606)873-1102. Wine and beer are available, dress is casual, and reservations are accepted. MC,V. ($)

UPTOWN CHATTER PORK LOIN WITH CURRANT SAUCE

1/2 cup soy sauce	1 1/2 teaspoons
1/2 cup dry sherry	dried thyme, crushed
2 cloves garlic, minced	4 to 5 pound
1 Tablespoon	pork loin roast, boned,
dry mustard	rolled, and tied
1 teaspoon ground ginger	Currant Sauce

Mix first 6 ingredients. Place roast in clear plastic bag; pour marinade in bag, close, and marinate overnight in refrigerator. Press bag against meat occasionally to distribute marinade. Remove meat from bag and place on rack in shallow pan; roast uncovered 2 1/2 to 3 hours at 325 degrees, basting with marinade during last hour. Serve with Currant Sauce. Serves 10 to 12.

For Currant Sauce: in saucepan, melt a 10-ounce jar currant jelly with 2 Tablespoons sherry and 1 Tablespoon soy sauce. Stir and simmer 2 minutes.

UPTOWN CHATTER
SPARERIBS WITH KRAUT

3 pounds pork spareribs
Salt and pepper
27-ounce can
  sauerkraut
1 cup chopped tart apple,
  (peel on)

1 cup shredded carrot
1 1/2 cups tomato juice
2 Tablespoons
  brown sugar
2 1/4 teaspoons
  caraway seed

Cut ribs in pieces; season. Place in Dutch oven and brown well. Combine kraut, including liquid, with remaining ingredients; spoon over ribs. Bake at 350 degrees, covered, 2 hours or until ribs are tender, basting with juices several times during last hour of cooking. Skim off excess fat. Serves 6.

UPTOWN CHATTER POTATO CASSEROLE

36 ounces frozen
  hash browns, thawed
8 ounces sour cream
1 1/2 teaspoons salt
1 1/2 teaspons pepper

1/4 cup chopped onion
One 10 3/4-ounce can
  cream of chicken soup
1 cup grated
  cheddar cheese

Mix all ingredients together and spread in casserole dish. Spread with topping and bake 1 hour at 350 degrees. May be prepared ahead and frozen for later use.

For topping: melt 1/2 cup butter or margarine in saucepan. Crush one tube Ritz™ crackers and mix with margarine.

TWO THIRTEEN ON MAIN
Danville

The Wilderness Road, hacked through canebrake and forest by Daniel Boone and his men in 1775, brought a steady influx of pioneers through Cumberland Gap, across the Cumberland, Rockcastle, and Dix Rivers, and into lands near the settlement at Harrodsburg.

Individual claimants to land established "stations" which served as islands of civilization, however crude, in the vast, dangerous woodland. They were not only home to the settling family, but served as defense against Indians, overnight stops for travelers, and trading posts.

By 1782, a number of stations encircled a plain between Clark's Run and Wilson's Run; one belonged to John Crow, who came to Harrodsburg in 1774 and to Danville in 1776. In 1884, he sold land to Walker Daniel on which the town of Danville was established.

Kentucky County, Virginia, became a district in 1783, but government administered from more than 500 miles away created difficulties. Frustrated by his inability to retaliate against Indian attack without consulting Virginia, Colonel Benjamin Logan called a convention of the Military Men of the District of Kentucky to meet at Danville.

This first Convention met in December of 1784, deciding to petition Virginia and Congress to make Kentucky a state. It took nine conventions and eight years, but in 1792, Kentucky became the first state west of the Alleghenies.

In Danville's Constitution Square, replicas and original early buildings mark the site of the Conventions. Much of the nearby business district was destroyed by fire in 1860, but the late-Victorian structures built on its ruins are a well-preserved representation of commercial architecture of the period.

A furniture store built in the late 1880s is most noticeable for heavy cast-iron "eyebrows" over arched windows on its two upper stories; it served as a funeral home, sporting goods store, and bridal shop, and, as part of Danville's Commercial District, was placed on the National Register in 1986.

Painted a sunny yellow with gray trim and green awning, Two Thirteen on Main is the outgrowth of a successful cheese shop/deli operated by Rick and Jane Brown a few doors down the street. The building, which had deteriorated, was renovated to bare walls, with new plumbing, electric service, heat, and air conditioning. Original tin ceilings were missing, offering the opportunity to install ductwork and create the unusual "skylight" ceiling above beautifully refinished original floors. The result is a bright, uncluttered, attractive restaurant, which has been equally successful with local patrons and visitors.

Taste is of prime consideration here, no matter what you order; Cream of Broccoli Soup is buttery and nicely textured, Chicken Cordon Bleu combines country ham and Swiss cheese, and yeasty little cloverleaf rolls are made fresh daily. Vegetables, too, are unexpectedly flavorful: English peas are cooked with mushrooms and oregano, sugar snap peas are crisp and green.

Desserts are real temptations; in addition to cheesecakes and Fresh Apple Cake, flaky homemade piecrusts might have fillings of chocolate, lemon, butterscotch, coconut, or chocolate pecan. Frozen peanut butter pie is marvelous.

Two Thirteen on Main is open for lunch 11 a.m. to 2 p.m., Monday through Saturday, and for dinner 6 to 9 p.m., Thursday through Saturday, and on the evenings of some weeknight performances at Norton Center. (606)236-1316. Danville is 9 miles southeast of Harrodsburg, about 35 miles southwest of Lexington via US 27 and KY 34. Dress is casual (some coats and ties in the evening) and reservations are preferred for dinner. No charge cards accepted; personal checks accepted. Busiest time is during Great American Brass Band Festival in mid-June. ($$)

TWO THIRTEEN ON MAIN
SPICY PEACH SALAD

20-ounce can sliced peaches	**1/2 teaspoon cinnamon**
1/2 cup sugar	**1/4 teaspoon cloves**
Two 3-ounce packages peach gelatin	**2 cups boiling water**
	4 Tablespoons vinegar

Drain peaches, reserving syrup and adding enough water to make 1 1/2 cups. Dissolve sugar, gelatin, and spices in boiling water; stir in reserved syrup and vinegar. Chill in 6-cup mold until gelatin begins to thicken; add peaches.

TWO THIRTEEN ON MAIN
ASPARAGUS SALAD

3/4 cup sugar
1 cup water
1/2 cup vinegar
3 envelopes unflavored
  gelatin, softened in a
  little cold water
2 teaspoons
  grated onion with juice

2 Tablespoons
  lemon juice
Dash salt
Two 10 1/2-ounce cans
  asparagus pieces,
  drained
2 pimientos, chopped
1/2 cup chopped pecans,
  toasted

In saucepan, blend sugar, water, and vinegar; boil 5 minutes. Dissolve softened gelatin in liquid, and add onion, lemon juice, and salt. In mold sprayed with vegetable spray, alternate layers of asparagus, pimientos, and pecans. Pour liquid over ingredients; refrigerate until set. Serve on a bed of lettuce.

TWO THIRTEEN ON MAIN DATE FINGERS

4 ounces butter
1 cup sugar
2 eggs, beaten
1 cup chopped dates
1 teaspoon vanilla

1 cup chopped pecans
3 cups Rice Krispies™
  cereal
Powdered sugar

In saucepan, melt butter, add sugar, eggs, and dates. Bring slowly to boil; lower heat and cook 10 minutes, stirring often. Remove from heat, add vanilla, pecans, and cereal. Cool and shape into fingers, then roll in powdered sugar.

THE TEA LEAF
Danville

One of the first structures in any pioneer settlement was a meeting house, and one is known to have existed on the Danville Square before 1784. The Concord church, one of three founded by Dr. David Rice, met here, and a larger structure was under construction by 1789.

Due to his Abolitionist convictions, Dr. Rice was unpopular with his congregation, and moved out of the area in 1798. The log church was replaced by a small brick church about 1812, and had 200 members by 1827. The church building now known as the "Presbyterian Church of Danville" was built next door to it, and the congregation moved in about 1832.

Education, no less than religion, was crucial to civilize raw frontier towns, and in 1819, the Kentucky Legislature chartered Centre College to be built near Danville. It grew slowly until the presidency was assumed by Dr. John C. Young in 1830. In his 27 years at Centre, attendance and curriculum advanced, and many graduates achieved national importance.

In 1834, Dr. Young was asked to be temporary pastor of the Presbyterian Church. He remained with the church eighteen years, during which the congregation grew dramatically. Expansion became necessary, and The Second Presbyterian Church was built at the corner of Third Street and Broadway, at which time the name "First" was assumed by the older church.

The sanctuary was in use by 1853; severely damaged in the fire that destroyed downtown Danville in 1860, it was rebuilt in 1862 in a Gothic style. The congregation consolidated with the First Church in 1969, and as part of the Lexington Avenue/Broadway Historic District, the building was placed on the National Register in 1972. The first floor became an antiques mall, and the Tea Leaf tearoom was opened in basement classrooms in 1989.

Rosemary Hamblin and Jane Stevens, a teacher and a school librarian, had discussed a bookstore/tea room for several years, and early retirement made it possible. Entering through the side of the church building, the visitor is greeted by displays of books and a browse-able bookshop, and the fragrance of good, homemade food wafting down the hall from the dining room.

The Tea Leaf's version of Kentucky cooking is light, with lots of vegetables and fresh fruits, emphasizing nutrition as well as good taste, and filling enough for those who prefer their main meal mid-day. There are two special soups and two generous hot entrées each day, plus salads and sandwiches and homemade hot breads.

Favorites include Kentucky ham on whole wheat with honey mustard, frozen fruit salad plate with ham biscuits, and "whatever the special is," often a hot chicken salad or a tasty casserole "like Mother used to make."

Saturday brunch might include Garlic Cheese Grits, fresh broccoli, and fruit salad, with a hot ham biscuit and muffins. Afternoon tea provides assortments of muffins, cookies, and desserts, and, of course, there's always tea, iced or hot in your own cute teapot.

The Tea Leaf, 230 West Broadway, Danville, is open for lunch Tuesday through Friday, 11 a.m. to 2 p.m., for afternoon tea, 2 to 4 p.m., and for Saturday brunch, 11 a.m. to 2 p.m. It is closed two weeks in January. (606)236-7456. Dress is casual, although many guests dress up; reservations are preferred, and are necessary between 12 noon and 1 p.m.; and there is an outdoor "café" when weather permits. No charge cards accepted; personal checks accepted. Busiest time is during Great American Brass Band Festival in Mid-June. ($)

THE TEA LEAF HONEY OATMEAL BREAD

4 ounces margarine	**4 cups flour**
2 cups milk	**2 packets dry yeast**
2 teaspoons salt	**2 cups oatmeal**
1/2 cup honey	**2 eggs, beaten**
	1 cup whole wheat flour

In saucepan, melt first 4 ingredients and cool to lukewarm. In large bowl of mixer, mix flour, yeast, and oatmeal; add eggs and liquid mixture and beat on low speed until well mixed. Stir in flour until blended. Let rise until double; punch down and form into 6 mini- loaves. Let rise in pans and bake at 350 degrees 15 to 20 minutes. Cool on wire rack.

THE TEA LEAF PUMPKIN-CHIP MUFFINS

1 2/3 cups flour
3/4 cup sugar
3/4 cup mini-chocolate
  chips
1 1/2 teaspoons cinnamon
1 1/2 teaspoons
  baking soda
1/2 teaspoon nutmeg
1/2 teaspoon cloves

1/4 teaspoon
  baking powder
1/4 teaspoon salt
2 eggs
1/2 cup cooked pumpkin
1/2 cup melted butter
1/4 cup milk
1/2 teaspoon vanilla

In large bowl, combine first nine ingredients. Whisk together remaining ingredients, and stir into dry ingredients until just blended. Spoon into 4 greased 2 1/2" miniature muffin pans. Bake at 350 degrees about 15 minutes. Yields 48 tiny muffins.

Chef's note: grated FRESH orange zest adds great flavor.

THE TEA LEAF FROZEN FRUIT SALAD

16-ounce package frozen
  strawberries, thawed
1/4 cup frozen orange
  juice concentrate
16-ounce can apricots

20-ounce can
  crushed pineapple
Juice of 1 lemon
3 bananas, chopped
Nuts

Mix fruits and juices together; add nuts, and freeze. Keeps well in freezer.

THE SHAKER VILLAGE OF
PLEASANT HILL
near Harrodsburg

$\mathbf{I}$n this charming community, thirty nineteenth-century buildings have been restored on 2700 acres of beautiful rolling farmland, the largest and most complete of any Shaker colony still in existence.

A National Landmark from boundary to boundary, "Shakertown" was one of 18 Shaker communities founded during the late eighteenth and early nineteenth centuries.

The United Society of Believers in Christ's Second Appearing called themselves "Believers," but were known as "Shakers" due to the dance-like form of their religious services. Individuals from many backgrounds gave up families and possessions to live apart from "the world" in an environment of sexual and racial equality. Shakers were celibate, industrious people, who dedicated their lives to hard work and superior craftsmanship. Their colony at Pleasant Hill endured a little over a hundred years, closing in 1910; the last Kentucky Shaker died in 1923.

Evidences of their work remain at Pleasant Hill today in original Shaker furniture, elegant and unornamented; hundreds of Shaker tools; and the buildings themselves, a very Southern adaptation of Georgian-Federal architecture.

In the restored buildings, interpreters in Shaker dress explain the strange, productive lives of the Shakers, and demonstrate Shaker crafts, including the making of the famous Shaker flat broom. During Shaker Heritage Weekends each September, additional programs of music, dance, cooking, and crafts are scheduled.

The serenity and calm of Shakertown may be enjoyed for an hour or two, overnight, or for days; lodging is available in fifteen historic buildings. From Shaker Landing, riverboat rides on The Dixie Belle offer a spectacular view of the Kentucky River's limestone cliffs.

Visitors have always been welcomed to the three-story brick Trustees' House, where electric candles gleam in cherry sconces suspended from Shaker peg-rails, simple muslin curtains tall windows, rag carpets cushion floors, and twin staircases spiral upward in simple beauty. In the dining rooms, Shaker-designed tables are bare, and low chairs slide beneath with typical Shaker efficiency.

Regional Kentucky foods, seasonal favorites, and Shaker specialties are offered at the table by servers in Shaker dress, with no limit to "helpings" of the delicious fresh vegetables and hot breads which accompany each meal.

No one leaves Shakertown hungry; full though you may be, you are cautioned to "Shaker your plate," and like Pleasant Hill's original residents, leave nothing to waste.

The Shaker Village of Pleasant Hill is on US 68, 25 miles southwest of Lexington and 7 miles northeast of Harrodsburg. (606)734-5411. Three meals a day are served in seatings; reservations are strongly advised. Dress is casual, and there is a strict no-tipping policy. There are 77 overnight units. MC,V. ($$)

PLEASANT HILL
EGG IN ASPIC ON ANCHOVY TOAST*

1 teaspoon gelatin	3 hard-cooked eggs,
1/2 cup water	halved
1 1/2 cups hot, canned	Toast rounds
beef consommé	Anchovy paste
1 1/2 teaspoons	Mayonnaise
lemon juice	

Sprinkle gelatin on water; pour on hot consommé and mix. Add lemon juice. Cool and pour 1/2 inch into six 1 1/2-inch deep individual molds. Place 1/2 egg, cut side up, in each and chill until firm. Add remaining consommé and chill. Serve on toast spread with anchovy paste; top with mayonnaise, thinned slightly with milk and seasoned with lemon juice and Tabasco™ sauce. Serves 6.

Note: additional gelatin may be added if a firmer aspic is preferred.

PLEASANT HILL CHICKEN KEENE*

1/3 cup butter
1/3 cup flour
1 cup chicken broth
1 1/2 cups milk or cream
2 teaspoons salt
1/8 teaspoon pepper
Meat from 1 cooked hen,
  cubed

1/2 pound mushrooms,
  sliced
1 pimiento in strips
1 green pepper in strips
Sherry wine to taste
Tart or patty shells
Paprika

In double boiler, melt butter; stir in flour. Gradually add liquids, stirring until thickened. Season. Add chicken, vegetables, and sherry. Serve in shells, and sprinkle with paprika. Serves 8.

PLEASANT HILL LEMON BREAD**

1/3 cup shortening
1 cup sugar
2 eggs
1 1/2 cups flour, sifted
1 1/2 teaspoons
  baking powder

1/4 teaspoon salt
1/2 cup milk
Grated rind of 1 lemon
1/2 cup chopped nuts

In large bowl of mixer, cream shortening with sugar until fluffy. Beat in eggs, one at a time, then dry ingredients alternately with milk. Add rind and nuts. Pour into 1 large greased loaf pan or 2 small ones. Bake at 350 degrees about 60 minutes. Pour on glaze and cool.
For glaze: mix juice of 1 lemon with 1/3 cup sugar.

BEAUMONT INN
Harrodsburg

T he oldest permanent settlement west of the Alleghenies, Harrodsburg was founded in June, 1774. James Harrod and 30 companions paddled down the Monongahela and Ohio rivers and up the Kentucky River, then trekked overland to Big Spring, where they built a fort.

Women and children arrived in the fall of 1775, bringing civilization to the wilderness, and the outpost rapidly grew into a gracious town, known for its culture and social life.

Among the many handsome Greek Revival structures remaining in Harrodsburg is white-columned Beaumont Inn, built in the 1840s as a boarding school. Superior young ladies knew it as Greenville Female Institute, Daughters' College, and Beaumont College, all unusual institutions in which academically oriented curricula rivaled those in men's colleges of the period.

The school continued in successful operation until 1914, when its president and owner died. In 1918, Annie Bell Goddard, a graduate of Daughters' College and former dean of Beaumont College, opened Beaumont Inn, converting the college's spacious rooms into a country inn of great distinction. Placed on the National Register of Historic Places in 1980, it is now operated by the third and fourth generations of her family.

Beaumont Inn is the focal point of 30 wooded acres; three buildings on the grounds serve as additional guest houses, their rooms filled with antiques, many of which are family pieces. Here may be found the relaxation and comfort of an earlier age, with the modern pleasures of swimming, golf, and tennis.

Guests are welcomed to Beaumont Inn in a front hall filled with memorabilia of General Robert E. Lee, and may meet friends in a double parlor furnished with period antiques. The reception area is in the former school library, in which old books may still be seen. Large dining rooms in gold, green, and pumpkin colors are settings for arrangements of fruits, vegetables, and flowers, depending upon the season, but the famous traditional Kentucky fare is the stellar attraction.

Fried "yellow-legged" chicken and carefully aged country ham top a menu of Southern favorites, and these, plus a daily special entrée, are accompanied by appetizer, salad, vegetables (including their renowned corn pudding), and homemade biscuits. Among old-fashioned dessert delights are their famous Robert E. Lee and Chocolate Sherry cakes, fruits in meringues and cobblers, Fig Pudding, and Huguenot Torte.

Beaumont Inn, 638 Beaumont Drive, Harrodsburg, is open from mid-March until mid-December. Breakfast is served only to overnight guests, and lunch seatings are at 12 noon and 1:15 p.m., Tuesday through Saturday, 12 noon and 1:30 p.m., Sunday. Dinner seatings are 6 and 7:30 p.m., Monday through Saturday, and 6 p.m. only on Sunday. (606)734-3381. Harrodsburg is about 35 miles southwest of Lexington via US 68 or the Bluegrass Parkway and US 127. Dress is casual (shorts not allowed in evenings or Sunday) and reservations are strongly advised. There are 33 overnight units. AE,MC,V. ($$)

BEAUMONT INN WHITE HOUSE DRESSING*
for green salads

1 cup sugar	3 Tablespoons
1 cup white vinegar	yellow mustard
1 cup vegetable oil	3 Tablespoons
1 green sweet pepper	coarse salt
2-ounce can pimientos	3 Tablespoons
1 medium onion	Worcestershire sauce

Blend sugar with vinegar and oil until dissolved. Grind vegetables together and combine all ingredients. Let stand 3 hours. Keeps indefinitely, if refrigerated. Yields 1 quart.

BEAUMONT INN
LIBBY'S HURRY-UP CHICKEN*

**Four 4-ounce boneless
chicken breast halves
1/4 cup Italian salad
dressing**

**1/3 cup Italian seasoned
dry bread crumbs**

Dip chicken in dressing, roll in bread crumbs, and place in baking dish. Cover and bake at 450 degrees; uncover and bake 10 additional minutes.

BEAUMONT INN ZUCCHINI CHARLOTTE*

**3 cups cubed zucchini
1 green pepper,
finely diced
16 ounces tomato juice
4 ounces chili sauce**

**2/3 cup flour/water
mixture for
thickening
1 cup grated
American cheese**

In pot of water, boil zucchini and pepper until tender. Drain. In double boiler, heat tomato juice and chili sauce; add thickening and stir until consistency of heavy cream. Stir in cheese, then vegetables, and heat. Serves 8.

BEAUMONT INN APPLE BROWN BETTY*

**4 Delicious apples
(red or golden),
peeled and sliced
2 cups bread crumbs
1 1/2 cups sugar**

**1/2 cup melted butter
Juice of 1 large orange,
with water to
make 2/3 cup**

In greased baking dish, layer apples, crumbs, sugar, butter, and juice mixture; repeat. Cover and bake at 350 degrees 45 minutes. Serve in individual saucers, topped with whipped cream or ice cream. Serves 6 to 8.

*From BEAUMONT INN SPECIAL RECIPES Harrodsburg, Kentucky. Used by permission.

RICK'S CITY CAFÉ
Frankfort

Generations of American school children, raised on tales of the treachery of Benedict Arnold and Aaron Burr, have scarcely heard of James Wilkinson, whose perfidy outstrips the two combined. Largely undetected during his lifetime, his story lacks the necessary moral.

Wilkinson arrived in Kentucky in 1784, a Revolutionary War Brigadier General who had married one of the Philadelphia Biddles. Tall, handsome, and plausible, he was a merchant and salt broker of dubious background and limitless ambition. He purchased land on the Kentucky River that became the original site of Frankfort. The street intended to be the town's major thoroughfare he named "Wilkinson;" Ann Street honored his wife.

In 1787, Wilkinson took a flotilla of flatboats loaded with Kentucky products downriver to New Orleans, and successfully negotiated their sale with Spanish officials. Kentuckians, excited at the prospect of increased commerce, failed to notice he monopolized all future trade. In less public bargains with the Spanish, in which he agreed to separate Kentucky from Virginia and from the Union, Wilkinson swore allegiance to the Spanish crown, and accepted money for his treasonous services for years.

On Frankfort's original plat, the third north/south street dead-ended into the (Old) Capitol grounds, and was named for General Arthur St. Clair, hero of Quebec. Lined with commercial structures built to replace those lost in an 1870 fire, the street was closed to traffic and made into a pedestrian mall in 1974.

On the west side of the mall, a three-story, five-bay Second Empire-style building constructed in 1871 is part of a complex of buildings that has had many uses. With the Frankfort Commercial District, it was placed on the National Register in 1979.

The little building had stood vacant several years when it was adapted as a restaurant in the early 1980s. Rick Paul, a classically trained chef who worked there, left to cook on two famous horse farms; when the opportunity arose to have his own restaurant, he returned to open Rick's City Café.

A relaxed, highly original restaurant, Rick's is not only unlike anywhere else, it can be many different places, depending upon when you visit. On a pleasant day, you can have lunch on the tree-shaded mall and watch the outdoor grill turn out your grilled chicken, cheeseburger, or Cajun ribeye sandwich. If you prefer air-conditioning, there's a full menu inside, with superb gumbo, salads, and sandwiches such as Rick's Muffaletta (Genoa salami, ham, olives, and vegetables on a French roll, topped with melted Swiss cheese), Monte Cristo, and Kentucky Hot Brown.

Rick's interests center on spices, garlic, totally fresh, and homemade on the spot; you won't find bland, processed foods here. French bread, pita bread, soups, sauces, salad dressings—in short, everything—is made here, and made well. There's a definite New Orleans influence, some Italian dishes, and on Friday nights, farm-raised, freshwater catfish.

The only constant at Rick's City Café is quality: menu offerings are always changing; entertainment, often Jazz or Blues, varies with the performer and attracts different crowds; and even the atmosphere seems to adapt to what's going on.

The food is always outstanding.

Rick's City Café, 325 Saint Clair Mall, Frankfort, is open for lunch Monday through Friday, 11 a.m. to 2 p.m.; for Karaoke performance night on Wednesday, 8 p.m. to 12 midnight, with a light menu; frequently on Thursday for live theatre with a special menu; and for dinner 6 to 10 p.m. on Friday and Saturday. (502)223-5525. All legal beverages are available, dress is casual, and reservations are accepted for theatre nights only, when they are strongly suggested. AE,MC,V. ($$)

RICK'S CITY CAFÉ
MUSHROOM CLAM BISQUE

8 ounces butter (2 sticks)	**1 1/2 teaspoons**
1/2 onion, chopped	**minced garlic**
Mushrooms	**Tabasco™**
1 cup flour	**1 Tablespoon**
3 quarts chicken stock	**Worcestershire sauce**
Chopped canned clams	**1 cup half-and-half cream**
Salt and pepper	**Small amount**
	tomato juice

In large stockpot, melt butter and sauté onion and mushrooms; stir in remaining ingredients in order given and simmer until done. Yields about 12 servings.

RICK'S CITY CAFÉ CHICKEN AND ANDOUILLE SAUSAGE JAMBALAYA

1 cup chopped
  green pepper
1 cup chopped celery
1 cup chopped onion
1 Tablespoon
  minced garlic
1/2 pound uncooked
  andouille sausage, in
  bite-sized pieces
1 cup cooked boneless,
  skinless chicken pieces
Worcestershire sauce
1/2 teaspoon basil
1/2 teaspoon thyme
2 bay leaves

1/8 teaspoon cinnamon
3/4 teaspoon
  chili powder
1 Tablespoon
  garlic powder
1 1/2 teaspoons
  black pepper
Salt
2 teaspoons
  cayenne pepper
1 cup peeled,
  chopped tomatoes
2 cups chicken stock
1 Tablespoon
  unsalted butter

Sauté green pepper, celery and onion. Add garlic, sausage and chicken. Season with next 10 ingredients; add tomatoes and stock. Simmer 1 hour or until sausage is done. Add butter. Serve over seasoned rice. Serves 4.

RICK'S CITY CAFÉ LINGUINE ALFREDO

For each serving:
1 Tablespoon olive oil
1 teaspoon minced garlic
Cooked linguine
1 or 2 Tablespoons
  freshly grated
  Parmesan cheese

1 or 2 ounces
  half-and-half cream
Salt and freshly
  ground pepper

In skillet, heat oil and sauté garlic. Add linguine and cheese; stir in cream and seasonings, and heat thoroughly. Serve with fresh garden salad.

CARROLLTON INN
Carrollton

The point at which the Kentucky River flows into the Ohio was an important landing place during Kentucky's early years. Indians knew the beautiful valley for its good hunting, and the rivers for transportation through the dense forest.

James McBride, traveling by canoe from Pittsburgh, carved his name into a tree around 1754, and is believed to have been the first white man in this part of the country. Simon Kenton came to hunt and stayed a few months, and James Harrod and his group stopped on their way to settle Harrodsburg in 1774. The point was permanently settled in 1790, when General (later Governor) Charles Scott and his Kentucky Volunteers built a blockhouse. Families who settled then are still represented in the area, and enjoy some of the loveliest scenery in the state.

The little settlement, first called Port William, was renamed when the county was re-divided in 1838, and county and county seat were named for Charles Carroll of Carrollton, Maryland, a signer of the Declaration of Independence.

Carrollton's most prosperous years came with the growth of river traffic. By 1794 there was regular boat traffic out of Pittsburgh on the Ohio, with the journey to Louisville requiring ten days, to New Orleans, 75 days. Despite Indian ambush and river disasters, the romantic riverboat era had begun; thousands earned their living on the Ohio, and to even greater numbers, the river was the highway to a new land.

Colorful river people, ranging from raftsmen and flatboat men to captains of luxury steamboats, found Carrollton a pleasant place to stop. Riverboat captains established comfortable homes and private clubs, and Houghton House was built in 1884 as a fine hotel catering to steamboat passengers. Three stories high, with plenty of guest rooms and a gracious dining room, the sturdy brick structure faced the Ohio river across a shady street.

Following several lean years, the building was restored in 1982, and once again welcomes travelers from Indianapolis, Louisville and Cincinnati. They come by road and by river, some just to sample the good food for which The Carrollton Inn is known, others staying several days to visit the historic town, placed on the National Register in 1982, or to ski or enjoy summer recreation at nearby General Butler State Park.

Carrollton Inn's comfortable dining room has grown to accommodate local and visiting guests who enjoy the 1880s atmosphere and small-town hospitality. Decorated in gentle shades of mauve, with tall windows overlooking the street, it is the scene of three generous meals each day.

Lunch includes crisp salads, juicy burgers, and generous sandwiches, plus different homemade soups every day—Cream of Broccoli and Seafood Chowder are popular—and lunch and dinner combination plates might feature homemade meat loaf, roast pork with apples, or baked chicken.

Home-baked loaves of honey wheat bread are passed, with serve-yourself big bowls of salad; steaks are hand-cut in the kitchen; there's always prime rib on weekends; and homemade desserts are irresistible. After Chocolate Caramel Pecan Cheesecake, Mississippi Mud Cake, or Hot Fudge Cake with ice cream and fudge sauce, you'll feel as lazy as the Ohio River just outside.

Carrollton Inn, 218 Main Street (corner of 3rd), Carrollton, is open 6 a.m. to 10 p.m. Monday and Tuesday, until 11 p.m. Wednesday through Friday. Saturday hours are 7 a.m. to 11 p.m., and Sunday hours are 8 a.m. to 9 p.m., with continuous service daily. (502)732-6905. Carrollton is about 45 miles northeast of Louisville, about 60 miles southwest of Cincinnati, just 2 miles from I-71 on the Ohio River. Dress is casual, all legal beverages are available, and reservations are accepted, advisable on weekends or for overnight. There are 10 overnight rooms. AE, MC,V. ($$)

CARROLLTON INN SEAFOOD CHOWDER

1 cup butter or margarine	1/2 cup diced celery
1 cup flour	Salt and white pepper to taste
1 quart chicken stock or canned broth	1/2 teaspoon garlic
1 quart half-and-half cream	1 cup small shrimp, cooked, peeled, and deveined
1 cup diced potatoes	1 cup imitation crab meat pieces
1 cup diced carrots	

In large stockpot, melt butter, add flour, and cook over medium heat, stirring constantly, 3 to 4 minutes. Stir in stock and cream; if mixture is too thick, add water. Add vegetables and seasonings and cook until vegetables are almost tender; add seafood and cook a few more minutes.

CARROLLTON INN CAJUN CHICKEN

4 boneless
  chicken breast halves
Cajun seasoning
Oil for frying
12 ounces cream cheese

1 quart
  half-and-half cream
1/3 cup white wine
2 cups broccoli cuts
Salt

Sprinkle chicken breasts with seasoning according to taste; in skillet, fry in oil. In large pan, combine cream cheese, cream, and wine, and cook over medium heat, stirring with a wire whip, until mixture begins to thicken. Add broccoli and seasonings and cook until broccoli is tender. To serve, place chicken breast on rice or pasta and top with Cajun broccoli sauce. Serves 4; there will be sauce left over. Use on leftover rice or pasta later as a side dish.

CARROLLTON INN PINK LEMONADE PIE

9" graham cracker crust
8 ounces cream cheese,
  softened
14-ounce can sweetened
  condensed milk

1 packet pink
  lemonade mix
4 ounces
  whipped topping

In large bowl of mixer, blend cream cheese and sweetened condensed milk until smooth. Add lemonade mix and whipped topping. Fill pie shell and refrigerate 1 to 2 hours. May also be made with a meringue topping.

SCIENCE HILL INN
Shelbyville

When Julia Ann Tevis moved to Shelbyville with her Methodist clergyman husband in 1824, she opened Science Hill Female Academy, a school for girls which offered a real curriculum. The school was not expected to succeed—young ladies were considered to have little need of "boys' subjects": chemistry, mathematics, history, botany, rhetoric, and philosophy. Nevertheless, 20 students appeared on the first day, and immediate expansion began. A large dining room, dormitory class rooms and a chapel were added, for a total of 78 rooms surrounding a courtyard, which was enclosed in 1848.

By that time, there were more than 200 day and boarding pupils, from many states, and John Tevis had given up the ministry to become spiritual head of the school. Science Hill continued in operation until 1939 with only one change in ownership, maintaining an outstanding reputation for education.

The building was used for a time as a residential inn, and in 1947, Mark Scearce opened Wakefield-Scearce Galleries in the chapel, showing antiques, silver, and decorative accessories. In 1960, he bought the entire structure, and today the internationally known gallery shares the former school with six specialty shops and the popular restaurant, Science Hill Inn. It was placed on the National Register in 1975.

Science Hill Inn, operated since 1978 by Terry and Donna Gill, who were joined by their daughter Ellen in 1988, presents updated traditional Kentucky fare in the high-ceilinged Georgian dining room where good food has been served for 150 years.

Tall windows on two sides overlook shady old gardens, and fresh flowers and white linens gleam in the sunlight at lunch, when you'll find Kentucky Bibb lettuce salad (with artichoke hearts, turkey, cheese, and country ham), Kentucky trout, or elegant sandwiches, plus a choice of rich homemade desserts.

Evening entrées might be marinated lamb medallions with onion garlic jam, pork tenderloin scallops on red and green cabbage, shrimp Créole over corn, or veal chops and country ham in a port/mushroom sauce.

The Sunday buffet, served on silver from the Wakefield-Scearce vault, always offers fried chicken, country ham, and a third meat, accompanied by corn pudding and green beans with old ham. Frequently included are zucchini casserole, cauliflower with mustard mayonnaise, tomato pudding, cucumber mousse, and wild rice salad, with buttermilk biscuits and hot water corn bread. This is Kentucky hospitality at its best, and there's still dessert....

Science Hill Inn, 525 Washington Street, Shelbyville, is open for lunch Tuesday through Saturday, and for the Sunday buffet, 11:30 a.m. to 2:30 p.m. Dinner is 6 to 8:30 p.m., Thursday through Saturday. (502)633-2825. Shelbyville is 45 miles west of Lexington, 28 miles east of Louisville, via US 60 or I-64. Dress is casual, all legal beverages are served, and reservations are suggested, especially during November and December. AE, MC, V, personal checks. ($$)

SCIENCE HILL INN
CREAM OF TOMATO SOUP*

2 Tablespoons butter	Reserved juice
1 small onion,	from tomatoes
finely chopped	1 quart chicken stock
Three 1-pound cans	1/4 cup sugar
whole tomatoes,	1 pint cream
coarsely chopped	3 Tablespoons dill weed

In soup pot, melt butter and sauté onion until transparent. Add tomatoes, juice, stock, and sugar. Bring to boil; lower, add cream, and simmer 20 minutes. Add dill weed and serve.

SCIENCE HILL INN
BISCUIT PUDDING WITH BOURBON SAUCE*

Ten 1 1/2-inch biscuits	**2 Tablespoons vanilla**
1 quart milk	**2 Tablespoons**
6 eggs	**melted butter**
2 cups sugar	**Bourbon sauce**

Break biscuits into small pieces in large bowl. Add milk; soak 5 minutes. Beat eggs with sugar and vanilla and add to mixture. Pour melted butter into 2-quart baking dish, add pudding, and bake until set at 350 degrees (about 1 hour). Serve warm with bourbon sauce.

For bourbon sauce: melt 1 stick butter in heavy pan. Add 1 cup sugar and cook 5 minutes, stirring occasionally. Beat 1 egg in bowl, gradually adding butter mixture while whisking constantly. Add 1/3 cup bourbon and serve.

SCIENCE HILL BROWN SUGAR PIE*

One 9-inch unbaked	**3/4 cup melted butter**
pie shell	**3/4 cup**
1 pound light	**half-and-half cream**
brown sugar	**Whipped cream**
4 Tablespoons flour	
3 eggs	

In mixing bowl, combine sugar and flour. Beat in eggs one at a time. Gradually add butter and cream, mixing until well combined. Pour into pie shell and bake at 350 degrees 40 to 50 minutes. Serve warm, topped with slightly sweetened whipped cream. Serves 8.

*from DONNA GILL RECOMMENDS. Shelbyville, Kentucky. Used by permission.

OUR BEST RESTAURANT
Smithfield

The "Great Meadow" across the Appalachian ranges tempted Europeans in the over-farmed east from the 1750s, when it was first explored. Its fertile soil, numerous streams, springs and salt licks attracted game, which, in turn, brought hunters from many Indian tribes. None laid claim to it, returning to their own lands by the many trails that crossed it.

Delaware Indians, who had moved westward into the Ohio Valley about 1700, knew and used a mineral spring near the mouth of the Kentucky River. They were bribed to divulge its location to Jacob Drennon, one of a party of surveyors sent in 1773 by Virginia's Colonial Governor Dunmore. Drennon rushed ahead of his party to lay claim to the spot; Drennon's Lick and Drennon's Springs are important landmarks in early Kentucky history, and the latter became a fashionable resort in the mid-nineteenth century.

A few miles southwest, the little crossroads community of Smithfield was late in developing; it received its post office in 1851, and was named for Thomas Smith, President of the Louisville and Frankfort (later L and N) Railroad, who was responsible for having track laid through this part of Henry County.

By the mid-1880s, there was a mill in Smithfield, and ten years later, Richard Watkins replaced it with the present structure. Originally a steam plant with four sets of rollers, it was converted to electricity about 1930. Here, Our Best and Sunrise flour and Smithfield cornmeal were produced and distributed over a seven-county area, and by-product bran was sold to farmers as animal feed. The Smithfield Mill lasted through three generations, and closed in 1987.

Kenneth Way had loved the mill when he was a child, and when it came on the market, he bought it, plus rights to its flour and meal names and formulas. Long-range plans include a restaurant and demonstrations in the mill; for the present, flour and meal are being produced elsewhere to Smithfield Mill's formulas, and are sold at a restaurant temporarily housed in Smithfield's former post office, dating from 1850.

The little building had also served as a residence and a country grocery store; it was cleaned and refurbished and opened as "Our Best Restaurant" in September, 1990. Its eight tables are usually full at mealtime, drawing customers from Henry and surrounding counties who enjoy a pleasant excursion that terminates in good food. Menus are made from flour sacks, a carafe of ice tea is placed on your table, and the atmosphere encourages friendly conversation among tables of guests, many of whom know each other.

Kenneth and his wife Kay pride themselves on true country cooking, with a menu that uses bean soup (both white and brown) and fried corn bread (as good as you'll find) as a beginning. These appear at every meal, with other soups in winter. Green Pepper Soup (with smoked link sausage), steak soup, beef stew, and red beans and rice are frequent.

Specials might be pork chops, grilled chicken breast, country ham, or, occasionally, fried chicken livers or roast beef. These come with potato and a side dish, often green beans, corn, green peas, tossed green salad, or fresh fried apples.

There are hot biscuits anytime, made from Our Best flour, of course, which is also used for the marvelous flaky crusts on pies and cobblers. Be sure to save room for these; the chocolate meringue pie, rich and fudgey, may be the best you've ever eaten, and coconut, lemon, and butterscotch are equally popular. There are always blackberry, cherry, and peach cobblers, topped with two scoops of ice cream.

When you leave, you can take with you a stock of flour and cornmeal in a handy Our Best tote bag.

Our Best Restaurant, 5571 Railroad Avenue, Smithfield, is about 6 miles south of the Newcastle-Sligo exit off I-71, about 14 miles north of Shelbyville via KY 53 and 153. It is open 11 a.m. to 8 p.m. Tuesday through Thursday, plus Sunday, and 11 a.m. to 9 p.m. Friday and Saturday. (502)845-7682. Dress is casual, reservations are not taken, and charge cards are not accepted. ($)

OUR BEST BEAN SOUP
(given in Kay Way's words)

"This works well for both brown and white beans. Wash and pick through beans, discarding bad ones. Put beans in crock, cover with water and soak overnight. Drain and put in kettle, covering with clean water. Add salt to taste. I also like to add a dried red pepper pod. Bring to a boil, then turn fire down and cook until done. After beans have cooked about an hour, add country ham for seasoning. Serve with fried corn bread."

OUR BEST EGG CORN BREAD

2 cups
   self-rising cornmeal
2 eggs

2 cups cold milk
1/2 cup
   melted shortening

In bowl, place cornmeal; break eggs into cornmeal, add milk and shortening and stir together. Fry in well-greased skillet or griddle. May also be baked in greased skillet in hot oven.

TRAIN STATION RESTAURANT
Anchorage

Although the town of Anchorage was settled in 1783, it reached its peak a hundred years later, when residential areas were laid out according to a Frederick Law Olmstead design for a garden community.

Here, safe from the Yellow Fever and Malaria that threatened Louisville, wealthy people summered on spacious estates, while businessmen commuted from downtown, making Anchorage an early "bedroom town" for those who appreciated small town life, yet worked in Louisville.

One factor that made this kind of commuting feasible was the interurban railway, a phenomenon of the late nineteenth and early twentieth centuries, which reached its peak just before World War I. Thriving in the states of Ohio, Indiana, Illinois, and Michigan, interurban lines utilized electric traction cars—like long-distance streetcars with heavier, faster bodies—to connect towns by public transportation.

Indianapolis was considered the hub of eastern interurbans, and Louisville was a nearby center. The Louisville and Eastern Railroad had lines to such outlying towns as Okolona, Pleasure Ridge, Glenview, and Shelbyville. The line which reached Anchorage in 1901 terminated in a charming frame station built for both passengers and freight.

Like other interurbans, the Louisville and Eastern succumbed to competition from automobiles, and disappeared as rapidly as it had spread. The abandoned station served in several capacities, including dress shop and gift shop, and was placed on the National Register in 1980.

The little building often stood empty, but it became a restaurant in 1987, and owner Leonard Lusky increased the size of the building so skillfully that its original dimensions are hard to detect. He won the 1988 Historic Preservation Award for best commercial renovation in Jefferson County. This attention to detail is apparent in the food served in the Train Station, as well, with cosmopolitan treatments of highest quality ingredients.

Surrounded with art work, overlooking gardens and a lush "tropical deck" used for dining when weather permits, guests relax and enjoy beautifully presented, creatively prepared food. The menu changes frequently; recurring favorites include Shrimp Cortez (stuffed with Monterey jack cheese, wrapped in bacon in a spicy barbecue sauce) and

113

Newmarket Fillet of Certified Angus beef, served with Madeira and Béarnaise sauces.

Desserts are no less special; a summer favorite is Triple Berry Shortcake with Chantilly Crème. White Chocolate Mousse Torte is always divine, but beyond description is something called "Chocolate Inferno."

The Train Station Restaurant, 1500 Evergreen Road, Anchorage, is about 1 mile north of US 60, and is open Wednesday through Monday, 5 p.m. until 12 midnight. (502)245-7121. All legal beverages are available, dress is "tennis to tux," and reservations are suggested on weekends. AE,CB,DC,MC,V. ($$)

TRAIN STATION
SHRIMP AND CRAB FRITTERS

1 1/2 to 2 cups flour	2 pounds crabmeat,
1 Tablespoon salt	roughly chopped
1 Tablespoon	1/2 cup finely
white pepper	chopped celery
2 Tablespoons	1/2 cup finely
cayenne pepper	chopped onion
2 pounds shrimp,	4 eggs, lightly beaten
peeled, deveined,	Oil for frying
and roughly chopped	

Mix flour with seasonings. In large bowl, combine seafood, vegetables, and eggs; with wooden spoon (hands are best), mix in flour, being careful not to leave lumps. Mixture should be "gooey" but hold together. Use teaspoon to scoop golfball-sized fritters; deep fry or pan fry in 380 degree oil until golden brown. Avoid crowding; fritters may need to be fried in batches. Serves 8.

TRAIN STATION WARM BRIE SALAD

For dressing:
1/4 cup vegetable oil
1/4 cup olive oil
1/2 cup balsamic vinegar
2 Tablespoons honey

2 Tablespoons
  fresh oregano OR
1 Tablespoon dry
2 Tablespoons basil
1/2 teaspoon salt
1/2 teaspoon pepper

Blend ingredients well. Best if made at least 4 hours ahead. Mix again just before tossing with greens.

For Salad:
1 pound spinach,
  stemmed and cleaned
5 large mushrooms,
  sliced
1/4 red onion in
  thin rings or chopped

1/4 cup slivered
  toasted almonds
8 ounces Brie cheese,
  melted in 350 degree
  oven

In large bowl, toss all ingredients except cheese with dressing. Divide onto 4 plates, and top each salad with bits of warm Brie. Serves 4.

TRAIN STATION
MARINADE FOR TENDERLOIN

1 cup vegetable oil
1 cup soy sauce
3 Tablespoons honey
1 Tablespoon sesame oil
1 Tablespoon
  minced garlic

1 Tablespoon
  minced ginger
1 teaspoon
  red pepper pods

Combine all ingredients; in non-reactive container, marinate six 6-ounce portions tenderloin (or your choice of beef) for 2 to 4 hours, turning every 30 minutes. Do not marinate longer than 4 hours or beef will become too salty. Grill to taste.

OLD TALBOTT TAVERN
Bardstown

To the frontier traveler making his lonely way through the wilderness, the lights of a crossroads tavern were a welcome sight. Here he would find warmth, food, companionship, stabling for his horse, and a safe haven for the night. There would be news of the civilized world and the new country to the west, and perhaps even a precious newspaper.

Many taverns were little more than hospitable homes; others were authorized to "provide in said ordinary good wholesome food and lodging and drink for travelers," as stated in the 1785 tavern license, signed by Patrick Henry, which may be seen at Old Talbott Tavern.

Constructed at the intersection of important north-south and east-west trails in 1779, Old Talbott Tavern is believed to be the oldest continuously operating tavern in the country. It was placed on the National Register of Historic Places in 1973.

The original portion of the tavern, with stone walls two feet thick, faced east; a public room and kitchen were downstairs, and the upstairs was divided into quarters for men and women. Traces of the staircase may be seen in the taproom ceiling, where smoke-stained beams attest to two hundred years of use.

Visitors may lunch in this room, which served General George Rogers Clark as headquarters during the Revolution. Among other famous guests were Henry Clay, Andrew Jackson, William Henry Harrison, and Aaron Burr. Young Abraham Lincoln and his family stayed in the upstairs front room during a trial for ownership of the family farm; they lost, and moved to Indiana. Lodging is still available in that room and five others, each with its own interesting history and modern comforts.

Old Talbott Tavern has had a number of structural additions; a brick building similar to the original tavern was constructed parallel to it, and the courtyard between the two was enclosed to form the present lobby. Diners will enjoy the early 1800s Colonial Room, in which Queen Marie of Roumania had tea in 1926, and the upstairs room where, according to tradition, murals painted by companions of exiled King Louis Phillippe were defaced by Jesse James, who fired his pistols at the pictures.

Today, Old Talbott Tavern's foods reflect current

tastes, with a traditional flavor. Luncheon soups and salads are joined on the menu by country ham, beef, and seafood entrées; dinners feature Southern fried chicken, fried country ham, rabbit, and two chicken-ham combinations. Homemade breads and chess pie top off a generous meal.

Old Talbott Tavern, 107 West Stephen Foster, Bardstown, is open for lunch 11 a.m. to 5 p.m., Monday through Saturday, and for dinner from 5 to 9 p.m., Monday through Friday, to 10 p.m. Saturday. Seasonal Sunday service is 11:30 a.m. to 9 p.m. (502)348-3494. Bardstown is two miles off the Bluegrass Parkway, about 50 miles southwest of Lexington. Dress is casual, all legal beverages are available, and reservations are not necessary, but are requested for overnight guests. There are 6 overnight rooms in the tavern and 6 in another historic building. AE,MC,V. ($$)

OLD TALBOTT TAVERN
CHICKEN PHILLIPPE

For each serving:
2 boned chicken breast
  halves
Flour for dredging,
  seasoned with salt and
  pepper
Lard for frying
Worcestershire sauce

Poultry seasoning
Bay leaf
2 to 3 teaspoons red wine
  vinegar
1 Tablespoon brandy
1 to 2 Tablespoons
  Burgundy wine

Dredge chicken breast halves in seasoned flour; in skillet, braise chicken in lard until flour is browned. Place in oven-proof pan, sprinkle with Worcestershire sauce and poultry seasoning, and top with bay leaf and wine vinegar. Cover and bake at 350 degrees 15 minutes, uncover, remove from oven, and flame with brandy. Replace in oven when flame is out and cook an additional 5 minutes. Just before serving, ladle Burgundy on top. Serve on wild rice.

OLD TALBOTT TAVERN CORN FRITTERS

2 cups self-rising flour
1/4 teaspoon sugar
1 egg
1/4 cup canned whole
  kernel corn, drained

Milk
Deep oil for frying
Powdered sugar

In bowl, mix all ingredients, using just enough milk to moisten; batter should be stiff. Drop by tablespoon into deep oil at 325 degrees and fry to a golden brown. Roll in powdered sugar and serve warm.

OLD TALBOTT TAVERN PIE

One 9-inch
  baked pie shell
3/4 cup sugar
1/2 cup flour
1/4 teaspoon salt
1 1/4 cups water
2 egg yolks, beaten

1/2 cup orange juice
1 Tablespoon
  grated orange rind
2 Tablespoons
  lemon juice
Whipped cream

Combine sugar, flour, and salt in top of double boiler; add water, and stir until smooth. Cook and stir over direct heat for 5 minutes. Remove from heat, add yolks and cook 5 minutes longer over boiling water, stirring constantly. Remove from heat and add fruit juices and rind. Chill and turn into pie shell. Top with whipped cream. Serves 8.

Note: may also be topped with meringue.

LA TABERNA
Bardstown

St. Joseph's Proto-Cathedral, the first Roman Catholic cathedral west of the Alleghenies, was once the seat of a diocese that included the entire Northwest Territory. The cathedral, now designated a National Landmark, was completed in 1819, and that same year, St. Joseph's Southern Catholic College was established. Although the original college building was destroyed by fire in 1838, it was replaced almost immediately.

The new structure, named for Father Martin Spalding, was the main building of the college, first under parish priests, and after 1848, under the Jesuits. The school was closed during the War Between the States, but Spalding Hall was used as a hospital by both Union and Confederate forces.

After the war the school reopened as a seminary, and in the ensuing years it was again a college, an orphanage, and last a preparatory school, closing in 1968. Spalding Hall stood empty and badly in need of repair for two years; it was offered for community use, and the basement was renovated for a restaurant.

After six months of strenuous cleaning, followed by sand-blasting, the original brick arches without keystones were visible. The beautifully vaulted ceilings of what had been the boys' locker rooms and laundry became an unusual restaurant with a "wine cellar" feeling, with exposed rose-colored brick walls and a floor of solid bedrock. It was named "La Taberna," meaning a long hallway with arches, and opened in 1971.

Renovation of the entire building followed, and resulted in multiple occupancy; placed on the National Register in 1973, Spalding Hall also houses the Bardstown Historical Museum, the Oscar Getz Museum of Whiskey History, and the Bardstown Art Gallery.

La Taberna is not the easiest of these to locate; the entrance is on the side of the building, through wrought-iron gates and a long corridor, but it is worth the effort. Don't miss a peek at the banquet hall in the former chapel!

Purchased by Chef Nathan G. Shaw in 1988, La Taberna is a romantic, unusual restaurant lit by candlelight and a few wide windows overlooking the seasonal beer garden. Tablecloths and soft recorded music enhance the drama of food Chef Nathan describes as "Continental Eats," truly American cooking that includes input from classic cuisine and all the diverse cultures that make up this country, seasoned to his taste.

The same varied menu applies at lunch, dinner, and after-theatre, offering everything from burgers and sandwiches (try Chicken du Provence, seasoned with rosemary, lavender, and other herbs, topped with Provolone cheese) to handmade pastas to colossal servings of roasted prime rib.

There are always plenty of appetizers and special soups, and popular entrées include Tiger shrimp with handmade fettuccine in Alfredo sauce, Crispy Roasted Duck, and Mesquite Roasted Chicken basted with zesty barbecue sauce. Daily seafood specials might be Alaskan King Crab legs, Calamari, shrimp or shellfish in a piquant sauce, or Baltimore Crab Cakes. All entrées come with a crisp salad, fresh vegetable, and chewy homemade bread.

Among desserts are homemade apple pie, Derby Pie™, Kentucky Silk Pie™, and a variety of interesting cheesecakes.

La Taberna, 112 North 5th Street at Xavier Drive, Bardstown, is open Monday through Saturday, 11 a.m. to 1 a.m.; Sunday 11 a.m. to 2:30 p.m. and 5 to 6 p.m. All legal beverages are available, except Sunday, dress is casual, and reservations are accepted, but not required. AE,MC,V. ($$)

LA TABERNA CARROT SOUP AU CRÈME

5 to 8 medium carrots	3/4 teaspoon
2 quarts chicken stock	cayenne pepper
3/4 cup flour	1 1/2 Tablespoons
1 1/2 teaspoons paprika	minced garlic
1 1/2 teaspoons	1 quart heavy cream
dried powdered thyme	Whipped cream
1 1/2 teaspoons salt	Chopped parsley

In large stockpot, boil carrots in stock until tender. Drain, reserving stock; purée carrots in food processor with 2 cups stock. Add flour to processor with purée and blend well. Return stock to stockpot; whisk in carrot/flour purée and add spices and garlic. Boil until desired thickness, at least 10 minutes. Finish soup by adding heavy cream. Serve in bowls, garnished with a dollop of whipped cream and sprinkled with chopped parsley. Yields 1 gallon, about sixteen 8-ounce servings.

LA TABERNA
SUPRÊMES OF CHICKEN WELLINGTON

2 Tablespoons butter
1 pound
  fresh mushrooms
2 shallots, chopped
1 clove garlic, chopped
3 Tablespoons
  chopped parsley
1/4 teaspoon
  dried tarragon
Salt and pepper

Four 6-ounce whole
  boneless
  chicken breasts
  (do not split)
Pastry dough
1 egg yolk, beaten with
  1 Tablespoon water
Wellington Sauce
4 chicken livers, sautéed

In skillet, melt butter and sauté next 5 ingredients over high heat 5 to 8 minutes; season and chop in food processor. Do not over-process. Cool. Sauté chicken breasts and cool; divide mushroom mixture between chicken pieces, folding chicken to contain mixture. Wrap each breast in pastry dough and brush with egg/water mixture. Bake 10 minutes, or until pastry browns. Serve on a pool of Wellington sauce, garnished with sautéed liver. Serves 4.

For Wellington Sauce: In saucepan, boil 1 cup chicken stock, 1 cup beef stock, 1 Tablespoon finely chopped onion, and 1/2 teaspoon tarragon vinegar. Whisk in 1 Tablespoon flour mixed with 1 Tablespoon butter.

JOHN E's
Louisville

Revolutionary war hero George Hikes received land grants in Kentucky and settled near Louisville; his substantial acreage was later divided among his sons, and several of their houses still exist. One structure, believed to have been built about 1851 on the site of an earlier house, was a simple log cabin of two rooms downstairs and two up, with a dogtrot hall between.

The rough character of interior materials, recently exposed, leads to speculation that the house may have been built earlier for use as an outbuilding, and converted to a dwelling when the main house burned—walls of the house were constructed from hewn logs 14 to 18 inches wide. Outer walls were covered with clapboard and inner ones plastered, and although some additions were made, the house was relatively unchanged when it passed out of the Hikes family in 1947. A nearby cemetery contains graves of several members of this prominent Louisville family.

The house became a restaurant in the 1950s; the city had grown up around it, and the building had been expanded by further additions. Renovation has exposed the logs on some interior walls, and the four original rooms are now the core of a rambling restaurant which took its name, John E's, from two of the owners. It has been run by John and Penny Shanchuck and Ben and Barbara Edelen since 1983.

A patio, added in 1984, was so successful that it was enclosed for year-round use, providing an alternative ambiance and a setting for live entertainment on weekends.

John E's serves what its owners describe as "good old American food," comprised of such diverse items as Kentucky burgoo (a traditional stew), their very special steaks, and selections like rumaki, mahi-mahi, and celestial chicken, which remain from John Shanchuck's tenure at a Polynesian restaurant.

At lunch you'll find salads, sandwiches, and lighter entrées, while dinner specialties from the charcoal broiler include barbecued baby ribs, a steak and lobster combination, and the two-pound T-bone. These, plus nightly "Patio Specials"—catfish fillets or frog legs on Friday—and all-day Sunday features of fried chicken and roast beef, provide one of the best-rounded menus anywhere. Among desserts are homemade cheesecake and marvelous homemade black bottom pie.

John E's Restaurant, 3708 Bardstown Road, Louisville, is at the intersection of Hike's Lane, and is open 11:30 a.m. to 10 p.m. Monday through Thursday, until 11 p.m. Friday and Saturday, with continuous service; dinner menu begins at 4 p.m.. Sunday brunch is 11 a.m. to 4 p.m. (502)456-1111. Dress is casual, although shorts are not allowed; all legal beverages are available, and reservations, a good idea on weekends, are not accepted on the patio special nights. AE,DC,DS,MC,V. ($$)

JOHN E's MUSHROOMS IMPERIALE

12 extra-large
  mushrooms
2 Tablespoons margarine
2 1/2 ounces
  minced onion
2 ounces minced ham
3/4 teaspoon salt
1/8 teaspoon
  coarse black pepper
1/4 teaspoon
  monosodium glutamate

1/8 teaspoon oregano
1/8 teaspoon thyme
1/4 teaspoon
  Worcestershire sauce
1 ounce bread crumbs
1 1/2 ounces
  Burgundy wine
2 ounces margarine
2 ounces sherry wine
Hollandaise sauce*

Wash mushrooms; remove stems, set caps aside, and mince stems. In skillet, melt butter and sauté stems with next 9 ingredients. Add Burgundy and simmer 8 minutes. Fill caps with stuffing. When ready to serve, sauté in margarine, add sherry, and simmer 90 seconds. Remove to heat-proof plates, top each with Hollandaise, place under broiler, and heat but do not brown. Serves 4.

*Most general cookbooks have a recipe for this classic sauce.

JOHN E's SHRIMP SALAD

3/4 pound
small/medium shrimp
2 Tablespoons
lemon juice
3 hard cooked eggs,
diced
8 ounces celery,
diced 1/4 inch

3 ounces dill pickle,
chopped
3 ounces pimiento,
chopped
1 1/2 teaspoons salt
1 ounce
good mayonnaise

Peel, cook and devein shrimp; cut into 3/8" pieces. Place in bowl, add lemon juice, and mix. Add next 5 ingredients and mix well, then blend in mayonnaise.

JOHN E's SOUTHERN PEANUT BUTTER BRAN MUFFINS

2 cups bran
1 cup boiling water
1 1/2 cups golden raisins
1/2 cup rolled oats
1/2 cup wheat germ
2 cups plain yogurt or
buttermilk
2/3 cup honey
2 eggs
1/3 cup molasses

1/2 cup peanut butter
2 Tablespoons
safflower oil
1 cup whole wheat
pastry flour*, sifted
1 cup flour, sifted
1/2 cup soya flour*, sifted
2 1/2 teaspoons
baking soda
1/4 teaspoon salt

Combine first 5 ingredients in mixing bowl and let soften several minutes. In large bowl, mix next 6 ingredients. Stir in bran mixture, then blend in dry ingredients. Fill paper-lined muffin tins 3/4 full and bake at 375 degrees about 25 minutes. Yields 3 dozen.

*Available at health food stores

THE SEELBACH HOTEL
Louisville

After 25 years in the hotel business, Louis and Otto Seelbach were ready to dazzle the traveling world with a lavish new building. The year was 1905, and people of taste pampered themselves with every luxury; the "Grand Hotel," with its spacious lobby and sweeping stairway, was immediately popular.

Designed in Beaux-Arts Baroque, an architectural style incorporating elements of several historic periods, the hotel is impressive in its use of the finest materials and embellishments. The lower two stories are of Bowling Green Stone, the eight above of Harvard brick with stone trimming, and the soaring two-story lobby, with its murals and arched skylight of beveled glass, is walled and floored with marble.

Every amenity was made available to patrons: a special reception room for ladies; a rathskeller with vaulted ceiling, finished entirely in Rookwood tile; a magnificent billiard room paneled in mahogany; and a roof garden that could be enclosed in winter.

The heart of downtown Louisville moved south with the Seelbach; Fourth Avenue was an exclusive shopping district, and was used as a promenade by the fashionable for decades. With the decline of downtown (in Louisville and across the nation) The Seelbach fell on hard times, and frantic remodeling in an effort to attract business was often injudicious. Although many of the hotel's glorious features were obscured, they were not destroyed, and it was placed on the National Register in 1975.

Restoration, completed in 1982, exposed lobby murals hidden behind plaster and removed the false ceiling covering the vaulted ceiling. With the greatest care and attention to detail, The Seelbach was returned to The Age of Elegance.

The Oakroom, the Seelbach's flagship restaurant, occupies the former Gentlemen's Billiard Parlor, where hot and cold appetizers, exquisite soups and salads, and table-side preparation of fish, meat, and game entrées reflect the best of American contemporary cuisine.

Noteworthy are: shrimp cocktail, with huge shrimp, Grilled Heartland Vegetable Salad with Kentucky Bleu Cheese, and Australian Lobster Medallions in Basil Beurre Blanc.

The Café at the Seelbach is more casual and relaxed, offering homemade soups, creative salads—Seafood Salad in a Mason Jar—homemade pastas, sturdy burgers, and a batter-dipped Reuben Sandwich with Russian Dressing, all in the atmosphere of a country-French bistro. Delicious pastries are available to eat or to carry out.

The Seelbach Hotel is at 500 Fourth Avenue, Louisville, on the corner of Walnut; there is complimentary valet parking. (502)585-3200. Dinner in The Oakroom is 6 to 10 p.m., Monday through Friday, until 10:30 p.m. Saturday. Friday lunch buffet is 11:30 a.m. to 1:30 p.m.; Sunday brunch is 10 a.m. to 2 p.m. Coat and tie are preferred for men, and reservations are suggested. ($$$)

The Café at The Seelbach is open from 6:30 a.m. to 12 midnight, 7 days a week, with continuous service. Dress is casual, and reservations are not required. ($$) In both dining rooms, all legal beverages are available. AE,DC,DS,MC,V.

SEELBACH HOTEL
GRILLED HEARTLAND VEGETABLE SALAD

1 small zucchini, cut vertically	1 Tablespoon minced garlic
1 small yellow squash, cut vertically	2 ounces olive oil
	6 ounces mixed greens
10 shiitake mushroom caps	2 ounces bleu cheese crumbles
1 red bell pepper, in 1-inch strips	Tomato wedges
	Artichoke hearts

In bowl, marinate first 4 ingredients in garlic and oil 2 or 3 hours. Grill vegetables until half cooked; place on greens, sprinkle with cheese, and garnish with tomato wedges and artichoke hearts. Serve with cherry vinaigrette dressing. Serves 4.

SEELBACH HOTEL BAKED BRIE IN BRIOCHE

4-ounce wheel of brie
Two 6-inch squares of
  puff pastry
1 egg, lightly beaten

Sauce
Mandarin orange
  segments and mint for
garnish

Cut brie in half horizontally and completely wrap each half in pastry; brush with beaten egg. Place on baking sheet and bake at 350 degrees until golden brown. Ladle 2 ounces sauce on each of 2 plates and place brie on top. Garnish with Mandarin orange segments and mint. Serves 2.

For sauce: in saucepan, mix 1 cup red currant jelly, zest of 1/2 orange and 1/2 lemon, 1/2 teaspoon Cajun spice, and 1 ounce port wine. Add juice from citrus halves, and melt over low flame.

SEELBACH HOTEL
GRILLED CAPON WITH SWEET PEPPER
AND PAPAYA CHUTNEY

4 boned capon breasts
4 teaspoons olive oil
1/2 ounce fresh ginger
  in julienne

Chutney
Fresh basil OR fresh
  thyme

Marinate capon breast in oil and ginger for 5 or 6 hours. Grill. Place 5 or 6 Tablespoons chutney on each of 4 plates; place capon breast on top, and garnish with herbs. Serves 4.

For chutney: dice (1/4"): 1 red bell pepper, 1 yellow bell pepper, 1 green bell pepper, 1 papaya, 1 cucumber (peeled and seeded) and 1 tomato (seeded). In sauté pan, heat 1 ounce butter and sauté vegetables. Add 1 teaspoon ground red pepper and 3 ounces red wine vinegar. Simmer 10 or 15 minutes.

THE BROWN HOTEL
Louisville

In October, 1923, the town at the Falls of the Ohio went wild for a week; at the corner of Fourth and Broadway, the new Brown Hotel had opened, bringing Louisville into big-city status. The magnificent brick and stone edifice connected the downtown business district with residential areas south of Broadway, spurring continuing growth of an already thriving downtown.

Ten blocks of Broadway received new streetlights as part of the opening ceremonies; within five years, theatres, professional office buildings, parking garages and the bus depot were grouped around The Brown.

Combining several decorative motifs in its interior, The Brown was a personal expression of its owner, James Graham Brown, a Louisville businessman and philanthropist, who kept a watchful eye on everything that took place in the hotel.

Known for good food and comfort, the secret of The Brown's success was its outstanding, friendly service. Remembering its early days, former guests mention the elegance of the Bluegrass Room, the dark richness of The English Grill, and exciting private parties in the Crystal Ballroom. Then they reflect on the staff— real personalities who often stayed for decades—who made it possible.

During its years as a hotel The Brown welcomed celebrities and soldiers, dancers and debutantes, horse trainers and little ladies in white gloves. In the 1937 flood, with three feet of water in the lobby, it housed a thousand homeless people stranded by the high water, while the radio station on the 15th floor broadcast news and hope 24 hours a day.

When suburban growth caused the decline and then demise of The Brown, longtime employees and guests gathered to mourn before it closed in February, 1971. The building was used for a time by the Jefferson County Board of Education and was placed on the National Register in 1978, but shortly afterward, it stood vacant.

Downtown redevelopment slowly worked its way up Fourth Street, closed to automobile traffic in the early 1970s, and the Broadway Project Corporation, a non-profit organization, was formed in 1980 to improve the Broadway end of Fourth Street. Restoration of The Brown Hotel was part of an ambitious plan to restore a 3-block, 33-acre area that includes theatres, residential communities, offices, and retail space.

The NEW Brown opened in January, 1985, with guest rooms enlarged to modern standards. Fine food is again served in the beautifully paneled English Grill, and the Hot Brown Sandwich, a Kentucky institution that has been imitated and adapted by restaurants all over the country, is once more available in the place of its origin.

In addition to the Hot Brown (which is still popular) lunch in The English Grill features soups and salads, sandwiches, omelets, and hot entrées. The dinner menu is Continental, with hot and cold appetizers, special salads, and entrées of veal, duck or rack of spring lamb. Desserts for both meals, chosen from a cart, are unusual and delicious.

J. Graham's Café and Bar on Theatre Square is bright and open, overlooking the passing crowd on Fourth Avenue, and seasonal outdoor seating. Here you'll find a selection of appetizers, salads, and sandwiches (including the Hot Brown), with a daily soup/salad special and, at dinner, some appetizers in entrée portions.

The Brown Hotel, a Camberley Hotel, is at Fourth and Broadway, Louisville. (502)583-1234. Lunch in The English Grill is 11:30 a.m. to 3 p.m., Monday through Friday, excluding the summer months; dinner is 5:30 to 11 p.m., 7 days a week. Jackets are preferred for men, and jeans are not allowed; reservations are suggested. ($$$)

J. Graham's Café is open from 6:30 a.m. to 11 p.m., 7 days a week, with continuous service. Dress is casual, and reservations are not accepted. Complimentary hors d'oeuvres are available from 4 to 7:30 p.m. ($$) In all dining rooms, all beverages are served. AE,CB,DS,MC,V.

THE "ORIGINAL" HOT BROWN SANDWICH

4 ounces butter
6 Tablespoons flour
3 to 3 1/2 cups milk
6 Tablespoons grated
  Parmesan cheese
1 egg, beaten
1 ounce heavy cream,
  whipped

Salt and pepper
Sliced roasted
  turkey breast
12 slices toast
Grated Parmesan cheese
12 strips bacon

134

In skillet, melt butter; add flour and stir until absorbed. Stir in milk and cheese; add egg. Do not allow to boil. Remove from heat and fold in cream with seasonings. For each Hot Brown, place two slices toast on oven-proof dish. Cover with sliced turkey and sauce. Sprinkle with additional cheese and broil until speckled brown and bubbling. Remove from broiler, cross two strips bacon on top, and serve at once. Serves 6.

THE BROWN HOTEL
KENTUCKY LIMESTONE SALAD

1 head Kentucky Limestone (Bibb) lettuce
1 ounce bleu cheese, crumbled

1/2 ounce sweet red peppers in strips
Toasted pecans

Wash and dry lettuce. Cut bottom off head and shingle leaves around 2 or 3 plates. Top with cheese, peppers and pecans. Serve with Creamy Raspberry Dressing or Raspberry Vinaigrette. Serves 2 or 3.

BROWN HOTEL
CREAMY RASPBERRY DRESSING

4 ounces sour cream
4 ounces raspberry vinegar

3 ounces sugar
2 ounces bottled Melba Sauce

Place sour cream in bowl; whisk in remaining ingredients and chill 1 hour before serving. Serves 4.

THE OLD HOUSE
Louisville

At the end of the American Revolution, the northeast was plagued with overpopulation and exhausted soil, and many citizens had impoverished themselves by their support of the American cause. Migration to The West, particularly to fruitful Kentucky, offered a new beginning.

Like many another Pennsylvania family, the Rowans, William, Eliza, and their five children, floated down the Monongahela and Ohio rivers on a flatboat. They reached the Falls of the Ohio in March, 1773, after an arduous journey, and lived six years on property they owned on the Green River.

The Rowans moved to Bardstown in 1790, when John, the youngest son, was seventeen. He became a scholar, lawyer, orator, Congressman, Senator, and judge, and an enthusiastic supporter of education; he was one of the founders of the Louisville Medical Institute.

A shrewd businessman, John Rowan was a substantial landholder, whose Federal Hill, in Bardstown, is now My Old Kentucky Home State Park. He owned property in Ohio and Kentucky, with large holdings in Louisville, where he maintained a town house from 1823. It has long been believed that this house was the three-story Federal-style brick house at 432 South Fifth Street.

Constructed about 1830, the house was later owned by a family of dentists named Canine. Three generations of Drs. Canine lived and practiced in the house and brought many innovations to Louisville. "Rosepearl" celluloid was invented in the house, the first in Louisville to enjoy steam heat. Dr. Canine also wound his own dynamo and lighted the house with electricity, startling neighbors into calling the fire department.

Opened as a restaurant in 1946, The Old House was owned and operated by Erma Biesel Dick until her retirement in 1979; it was a favorite dining spot for local people and celebrities. After its closing, the building often stood empty, although several restaurants were attempted there, until it was taken over by Mike Francis in 1987.

Today it is a comfortably elegant place to have lunch, serving what Mike terms "old Louisville traditional food." Guests enter at the lower level, and may be seated in the rathskeller-like bar, or in two spacious high-ceilinged rooms on the first floor which are more formal, but far from stuffy.

On the third floor, a wall of stained glass panels from a demolished church in Memphis lights a large room often used for private parties.

Lunch at The Old House might begin with Burgundy Mushroom Soup or Seafood Gumbo, and go on to hot Prime Rib or Steak sandwiches (a 7-ounce New York Strip), Club or Chicken Salad Sandwiches, cheeseburgers, or a huge fillet of fresh codfish sandwich.

Popular salads include a Fruit Plate, with cottage cheese, chicken, or tuna salad, and the Club Salad—like a club sandwich in a bowl, with diced bacon, lettuce, tomato, and turkey. There are two hot entrées daily, each with salad and vegetable, and wonderful homemade desserts to choose from: Candy Bar Pie (melted Hershey Almond Bars™, whipped cream, and marshmallows),Irish Brownie (Chocolate fudge with Crème de Menthe and ice cream), and Kentucky Pie, a luscious chocolate chip pecan pie flavored with bourbon.

The Old House, 432 South 5th Street, Louisville, is open for lunch 11 a.m. to 2 p.m., Monday through Friday, and on occasional Saturdays and Evenings. (502)583-3643. All legal beverages are available, dress is "comfortable," and reservations are accepted. Busiest times are during Derby and Christmas seasons. AE,DC,MC,V. ($$)

THE OLD HOUSE CARROT SOUFFLÉ

2 cups cooked carrots	**1 teaspoon cinnamon**
2 ounces butter	**1 teaspoon**
3 eggs	**baking powder**
1 cup milk	**1/2 teaspoon salt**
1 cup sugar	**Nuts**
2 heaping	
Tablespoons flour	

Mash carrots with potato masher and add butter. Beat in eggs and milk; mix dry ingredients together and stir in with nuts. Pour into greased soufflé or baking dish and bake at 325 degrees for 1 hour.

THE OLD HOUSE IRISH BROWNIE

1 cup sugar	16-oz. can Hershey's™
4 ounces margarine	chocolate syrup
4 eggs	1 teaspoon vanilla
1 cup flour	Vanilla ice cream
1/2 teaspoon salt	Green Crème de Menthe

In large bowl, blend sugar and margarine; mix in eggs. Mix next 4 ingredients; add to first mixture and blend. Pour batter into greased 9" x 13" pan and bake at 350 degrees for 30 minutes—NO LONGER. Cool; pour on warm filling, cool again, and spread with glaze. To serve, cut into squares, top with vanilla ice cream and Crème de Menthe.

For filling: in saucepan, melt 4 ounces margarine over very low heat; beat in 2 cups powdered sugar and 4 Tablespoons non-alcoholic green Crème de Menthe.

For glaze: in saucepan, melt 6 Tablespoons margarine with 1 cup semi-sweet chocolate chips.

THE OLD HOUSE STRAWBERRY DESSERT

1 pound vanilla wafers	1 quart strawberries,
2 ounces butter, melted	cleaned and sliced
8 ounces butter, softened	1 pint heavy cream,
1 1/2 cups sugar	whipped
2 eggs	Whole strawberries

Crush vanilla wafers and mix with 2 ounces melted butter. Spread mixture firmly in 9" x 13" pan; save some crumbs to sprinkle on top. Cream softened butter with sugar and beat and beat and beat. Add eggs one at a time, beating well after each. Beating is MOST important. Spread mixture evenly over crumbs; top with sliced berries, then whipped cream. Sprinkle remaining crumbs on top and refrigerate overnight. Garnish with whole or halved strawberries. Cut into 15 pieces.

WHEELER'S ROADHOUSE
Louisville

Georposed George Rogers Clark was born near Charlottesville, Virginia, in 1752. At nineteen, a surveyor in Kentucky, he lived in the fort at Harrodsburg. His service in Lord Dunmore's War alerted him that England was arming Indians to attack American forts, and he traveled to Williamsburg seeking arms, money, and troops. At his instigation, Kentucky County, Virginia, was created in 1776.

Indian attacks increased during the Revolution; returning to Williamsburg in 1777, Clark obtained a commission as Lieutenant Colonel and secret orders from Governor Patrick Henry empowering him to attack British forts in the Northwest Territory.

In 1778, Colonel Clark, commanding inadequate troops and scantily provisioned, captured Kaskaskia, the main fort of Illinois, and enlisted its inhabitants. With their aid, he marched across frozen lands to take Vincennes, creating a new American boundary on the Mississippi. This increased the territory awarded to the United States at the Treaty of Paris in 1783, and made possible the 1803 Louisiana Purchase and the Lewis and Clark expedition, led by Clark's brother.

Without men and supplies needed to attack Detroit, Clark returned to The Falls, where he built Fort Nelson and laid out the city of Louisville. Neither he nor his men received any pay for their service, and Clark, never reimbursed by Virginia, was personally responsible for all expenses of the Northwest Expedition.

Betrayed by James Wilkinson (founder of Frankfort) who coveted Clark's military command in order to further his traitorous negotiations with Spain, General Clark was relieved of his command. Broken in health and spirit, impoverished by service to his country, "The Washington of the West" spent his last years in his sister's home, Locust Grove, near Louisville, where he died in 1818.

Just a few miles from Locust Grove, Cigvert Oyler built a simple two-story brick house on historic Beargrass Creek about 1869. Use as a multi-family dwelling barely changed its exterior appearance; a side porch was added about 1950. As a restaurant, its exposed-brick walls and open fireplaces create a pleasant country environment, enhanced by horse prints and softened with fabric swags on the ceilings.

The house, purchased in 1988 to expand Douglas Wheeler's successful vending-machine business, was intended to showcase the company's products, but evolved into a full-service restaurant. The menu includes traditional items such as Burgoo, Country Ham and Hot Browns, plus variations on Nouvelle and Classic dishes.

Soups, salads (grilled chicken, mandarin oranges, and pineapple on Bibb lettuce) and hot (Roast Beef on Rye with potatoes and gravy) and cold (Fancy Albacore Tuna salad on multi-grain bun) sandwiches served at lunch are available all day, joined in the evening by such entrées as Prime Rib, Country Baked Chicken and Grilled Halibut.

Nightly specials might be Boneless Breast of Duck with Black Currant Plum Sauce, Chicken Ravigote (stuffed with smoked Gouda and sautéed crab), Vegetable Lasagna, or Tenderloin in Bourbon Cream Sauce. Desserts often include Jeff Davis Pie, Bourbon Cake, fruit cobblers, and Grand Marnier Cake.

Wheeler's Roadhouse, 1765 Mellwood, Louisville, is at the intersection of Brownsboro Road, and is open 10 a.m. to 10 p.m., Monday through Thursday, 11 a.m. to 11 p.m., Friday, and 5 to 11 p.m., Saturday. (502)894-0723. All legal beverages are available, 70% of men wear coat and tie in the evening, and reservations are accepted. AE,MC,V. ($$)

WHEELER'S ROADHOUSE ASPARAGUS AND JALAPEÑO PEPPER CHEESE SOUP

1 pound trimmed asparagus	Roux
1/2 yellow onion, chopped	1/2 lb. jalapeño pepper cheese, shredded
1 Tablespoon chopped garlic	Cilantro
Vegetable oil for sautéeing	Tabasco™
1 quart chicken stock	1/2 teaspoon white pepper
	2 cups heavy cream

Poach asparagus. Reserving tips, run stems through food processor. Sauté onion and garlic in oil; add stock; drop in roux when stock boils. Add processed asparagus and cheese; season with cilantro, Tabasco™, and pepper. Add asparagus tips and cream. Serves 6.

For roux: blend 1 cup flour with 4 ounces softened butter.

WHEELER'S ROADHOUSE SPINACH SALAD WITH CARPACCIO OF TENDERLOIN

For each serving:
1 ounce tenderloin
Spinach, washed
  and stemmed
Raspberry Vinaigrette
1 medium egg,
  poached

Cream havarti cheese
2 strips bacon,
  crisply cooked
Orange and apple slices
Tomato wedges

Pound tenderloin thin between plastic wrap; grill; cut into julienne. Toss spinach in vinaigrette, place on plate, add tenderloin, and top with egg. Garnish with cheese, crumbled bacon, apple fans, 1/4 slices of orange, and tomato wedges. For Raspberry Vinaigrette: whisk 1 egg with 1/2 cup vegetable oil until thick; add juice of 1 lemon, 3 to 4 Tablespoons Raspberry vinegar, 1 teaspoon basil, and 1 Tablespoon honey.

WHEELER'S ROADHOUSE VEAL GORGONZOLA WITH CAPPACOLLA AND PORT WINE SAUCE

For each serving:
4 ounces veal, pounded
  thin and chilled
1 ounce cappacolla ham,
  thinly sliced

2 ounces
  Gorgonzola cheese
Port Wine Sauce
Toasted pine nuts

Roll veal around ham and cheese; sauté and place on oven-proof dish. Bake at 350 degrees 5 minutes; slice thin, and serve with sauce, garnished with pine nuts.

For Port Wine Sauce: in sauté pan with small amount of butter, sauté 1 shallot, choppped, and 1 clove garlic, chopped; add 1/2 cup port wine, flame, then 1 cup veal stock. Reduce by 1/2; add 1 Tablespoon butter.

PARISIAN PANTRY
Louisville

In eighteenth-century towns, baking was done in bake-shops, where housewives could purchase bread or take their own loaves and meats to be baked in large ovens. Isolated farms, where there might be several hundred workers, had bake-houses and cooks.

On the frontier, neither equipment nor flour were available. Cooking utensils were few and crude: a large iron pot for stews, a few wooden vessels, and perhaps some pewter plates. Large pieces of meat were roasted over an open fire; few homes had ovens of any kind.

Wild meat and corn bread were pioneer staples. Removed from the cob, kernels of dried corn were placed in a wooden mortar and pounded with a wooden pestle until finely ground. Mixed with water, the meal became Johnny cake (colloquial for "journey cake," because it traveled well), ash cake, corn pone, or mush, depending upon how it was prepared.

As life on the frontier became safer and more civilized, wheat was harvested and mills were built, and flour, although more expensive than cornmeal, was generally available. Baking was a necessary part of life and a respected skill, employed professionally when hamlets grew into towns, and towns into cities.

What is now the city of Louisville began as a group of frontier stations clustered near the Falls of the Ohio River; it was incorporated in 1780, when Kentucky County, Virginia was divided into Fayette, Lincoln, and Jefferson Counties. Although traffic on the Ohio increased Louisville's importance, more rapid expansion succeeded opening of the Louisville and Nashville railroad in 1859.

Residential and commercial growth followed established roads to outlying towns. The Bardstown Road, along the ridge of the Highlands, was already important before the area was settled, and periods of Louisville's development are indicated by architectural styles observed along the road.

A three-story brick commercial building with its entrance on the northwest corner of Bardstown Road and Bonnycastle Avenue lost its third story to a tornado in 1974. Probably built in the 1880s as a drugstore with the family living upstairs, it had been a book store and a record shop before becoming a bakery/restaurant in 1982. As part of the

Highlands Historic District, it was placed on the National Register in 1983.

Debbie Taylor, who took over Parisian Pantry in 1990, presents a bistro menu of over forty items, including pastas, salads, and entrées, while maintaining a real European bakery. You can relax over a cup of coffee and a pastry, enjoy a snack or afternoon tea, or dive into a full meal with equal comfort.

Special here are appetizers such as Shrimp Rèmoulade and Spinach Tapinade; entrées of homemade ravioli, or popular Curried Chicken Salad; or Black and Blue Sandwich (grilled chicken with Cajun spices and grilled ham with provolone).

There are always at least five fresh pastry choices— Zebra Cheesecake, fruit tarts in winter, and special cannolis— and more on weekends. They're available to carry out, as are four or more kinds of bread—French, wheat, Greek, Brioche, Challah—and "Gourmet to Go," a complete line of low-fat and fat-free products.

Parisian Pantry, 1582 Bardstown Road, Louisville, is at the corner of Bonnycastle Avenue, and is open 7:30 a.m. until 9 p.m., Tuesday, Wednesday, and Thursday; until 11 p.m. Friday and Saturday; and until 5 p.m. Sunday. The kitchen closes between 3 and 5 p.m., when only light fare is served. (502)452-6326. Wine and beer are available, dress is "a comfortable hodgepodge," and reservations are accepted only for parties of 6 or more. AE,MC,V. ($$)

PARISIAN PANTRY CAPELLINI AU PISTOU

6 ounces cream	**6 to 8 ounces**
4 ounces prepared pesto	**cooked capellini**
2 ounces freshly grated	**Toasted chopped**
Parmesan cheese	**almonds**

In sauté pan, place first 3 ingredients; reduce until thickened. Add capellini and heat through. Serve on warm plates, garnished with almonds. Serves 2.

PARISIAN PANTRY CHOCOLATE BREAD

2 packages dry yeast
2 Tablespoons sugar
1 cup warm water
1 1/2 cups
  unbleached flour
1 cup warm milk
3 Tablespoons melted
  unsalted butter
1 Tablespoon salt

4 to 4 1/2 cups
  unbleached flour
8 ounces
  semi-sweet chocolate
2 Tablespoons melted
  unsalted butter
3 Tablespoons
  powdered sugar

In large bowl, whisk together first 4 ingredients; cover and let stand in warm area until doubled, about 1 hour. Stir down; add next 3 ingredients and 1 cup flour and beat hard 2 minutes, or until smooth. Add flour, 1/2 cup at a time, until a soft dough is formed. Turn dough onto floured surface and knead 5 minutes, adding flour as necessary to keep dough from being sticky. Place in large greased bowl, turning to coat top, and cover. Let rise in warm area until doubled, about 1 hour. Grease eight 2 1/2" x 4" pans; divide chocolate into 8 portions; set aside. Punch down dough, turn out onto floured surface and divide into 8 portions. Pat each portion into 4" x 7" rectangle; place 1 ounce chocolate at short edge, and roll up (as jelly roll), pinching edges to seal. Shape each into loaf pan, cover, and let rise about 15 minutes; dough will almost double. Brush loaves with melted butter and sprinkle with powdered sugar. Bake at 375 degrees 20 to 25 minutes, or until light brown. Remove from pans and cool on racks until just warm. Yields 8 small loaves.

DEITRICH'S IN THE CRESCENT
Louisville

$\mathbf{F}$reemasonry in the United States began in the early eighteenth century, when Masons immigrated from the British Isles. In 1734, Benjamin Franklin was elected grand master of Pennsylvania Masons; many of this nation's most prominent citizens have been Masons.

By the 1850s, the ridge between forks of Beargrass Creek was crossed by the Shelbyville Pike (now Frankfort Avenue) and tracks of the Louisville and Frankfort Railroad. Commuters built homes along the tracks, and the area was named "Crescent Hill," when it was incorporated in 1884. Known as "the first railroad and mule-car suburb of Louisville," the railroad has been important throughout its history.

Across Frankfort Avenue from the railroad tracks, Crescent Hill Lodge Number 320 of the Free and Accepted Masons built their new lodge in 1927. The $80 thousand structure of yellow brick, banded by stone in a Greek key pattern, housed a 525-seat movie theatre, a real estate office, and a dry cleaners, with the Masonic Temple upstairs. As part of the Crescent Hill Historic District, it was placed on the National Register in 1982.

The Crescent Theatre was a family movie house with occasional vaudeville and magic acts, but by the mid-1980s, it had deteriorated into an X-rated theatre, which closed in 1987. In November, 1988, it was reopened as "Deitrich's in the Crescent," an American bistro with an unusual format and the exciting, creative food for which owner Bim Deitrich has been noted.

The building's exterior, enhanced by faux stone banding and columns on its west side, retains its former appearance. "Bistro Grill" appears on the marquee, and here patrons like to linger at seasonal sidewalk tables, sipping wine and waving at trains.

Inside, textured gray walls and spare decor heighten the theatricality of an exposed kitchen with a wood-burning grill. Graduated floor levels lead down to a sort of orchestra pit, where Chef "Chip" McPherson brings forth picture-perfect, savory dishes. This is not only great food IN a theatre, this is food AS theatre.

On a given night at Deitrich's you might find Peppered Salmon in Lemon Grass Beurre Blanc; Chicken stuffed with Goat Cheese and Fresh Herbs with Chardonnay Cream

Sauce; and Veal Liver and Onions with Grained Mustard Sauce, all including potato and vegetable. The array of appetizers is so tempting you might want to order several instead of an entrée.

Desserts, of course, are all wonderful, but White Chocolate Mousse Torte is magnificent: chocolate crust, white chocolate mousse, and dark chocolate ganache, with raspberry sauce to splash on top.

Deitrich's in the Crescent, 2862 Frankfort Avenue, Louisville, is open 7 nights a week, 5:30 to 11 p.m., Monday through Thursday, to 12 midnight Friday and Saturday, and to 10 p.m. Sunday. (502)897-6076. All legal beverages are served, dress is casual, and reservations are accepted only for large parties. AE,MC,V. ($$$)

DEITRICH'S MARYLAND CRAB CAKES WITH GINGER RÉMOULADE

1 to 1 1/2 pounds lump or backfin crab
1 cup heavy cream
1 sweet red pepper, cored and diced small
1 sweet yellow pepper, cored and diced small
2 green onions, chopped fine
Bread crumbs
1 cup mayonnaise
1/4 teaspoon white pepper
1/4 teaspoon granulated garlic
1/4 teaspoon fresh or powdered ginger
Dash Tabasco™
Flour for breading
Oil for frying

Pick over crab for shells. In skillet, reduce cream by 1/2; set aside or refrigerate to cool. In bowl, mix crab, cream, 1/2 the peppers and 1/2 the onion. Refrigerate. When chilled, add enough crumbs to bind mixture together. Form into 8 cakes, 2-3 ounces each, about 1/2" thick; refrigerate cakes until ready. For rémoulade: in bowl, mix mayonnaise with remaining peppers, onion, and all seasonings. Set aside. In large skillet, heat 1/4" oil to about 375 degrees. Lightly flour cakes and cook 2 to 2 1/2 minutes each side until golden brown. Place 2 on each of 4 plates on a pool of rémoulade. Serves 4.

DEITRICH'S LEMON-BRANDY CHICKEN
WITH OREGANO AND THYME

1 cup chicken stock
2 ounces brandy
Juice of 1 lemon
1 teaspoon fresh oregano
1 teaspoon fresh thyme
Pinch black pepper

2 to 2 1/2 pounds bone-
 less chicken breasts
Flour
Oil for sautéeing
2 Tablespoons butter

In bowl, mix first 6 ingredients and set aside. Lightly flour chicken breasts; in large skillet with about 1/8" oil, sauté chicken 2 to 2 1/2 minutes each side until light brown. Remove and drain chicken. Drain oil from skillet; add chicken stock mixture to skillet, lower heat, and cook 2 to 2 1/2 minutes or until liquid has thickened to a sauce. Remove from heat and whip in butter. Return chicken to sauce to coat; serve over rice. Serves 4.

DEITRICH'S GRILLED TENDERLOIN
WITH ROASTED GARLIC-ROSEMARY-
COGNAC SAUCE

1 whole trimmed tender-
 loin, about 3 pounds
Oil
3 or 4 cloves garlic,
 peeled
2 cups brown sauce

(or rich brown gravy)
1 Tablespoon chopped
 fresh rosemary
1 ounce butter
1 ounce flour
2 ounces cognac

Lightly coat tenderloin with oil; grill over open coals which have already reached their peak (more smoke flavor and less heat), rolling 1/4 turn every 2 minutes; 20 minutes will reach medium rare. In skillet just covered with oil, roast garlic, shaking pan, until softened. Chop fine. In saucepan, bring brown sauce to light boil; add garlic and rosemary and simmer 10 minutes. Blend butter with flour and whisk into sauce; cook together until thickened. Remove from heat and add cognac. Return to low heat. Slice tenderloin into 3 to 4 ounce medallions; lay 2 on each plate on a pool of sauce. Serves 6 or 8.

BACK HOME
Elizabethtown

Many people who settled Kentucky's Heartland had gathered at Pittsburgh, then floated down the Ohio River on flatboats. Some debarked at Maysville, making their way southwest by perilous overland routes; others were piloted over the Falls of the Ohio, landing at the mouth of the Salt River. Proceeding on foot, or by wagon if the primitive roads were passable, they arrived in lovely Severns valley, where trails crossed in the wilderness, and a triangular cluster of forts gave protection from Indians.

These three forts, built in 1779, were the only settlements between Louisville and the Green River; a little community formed near one of them was named "Elizabethtown" for the wife of its founder. Among those who settled there was young Thomas Lincoln, who had immigrated to Kentucky from Virginia with his parents. The Lincolns had taken land near the Falls of the Ohio, but after Tom's father, Abraham, was murdered by Indians, the family relocated to land on the Salt River.

Tom Lincoln, a carpenter, lived for a time in Elizabethtown with his bride Nancy Hanks. Their daughter Sarah was born there in 1807, and a year later they bought a small farm about eleven miles southeast of town. In a crude log cabin on Sinking Spring Farm, Abraham Lincoln was born on February 12, 1809.

By mid-1811, they had moved nine miles northeast, to Knob Creek. This was the first home Abraham Lincoln could remember, but a tragic one; threatened with debt, the family moved to Indiana in 1816, leaving a baby brother buried on Muldraugh's Hill near their home.

A few blocks from a cabin Thomas Lincoln helped remodel is a two-story red brick town house built in 1872. Although simple, the house has elements of Italianate design, and its overall effect is one of dignified prosperity. Long the residence of the Bryan family, it was later a dress shop, remaining in the family until 1989, when it was bought by Linda and Tommy Fulkerson to become a charming country craft and gift shop.

Although Linda never intended to go into the restaurant business, she did provide sandwiches and coffee to keep men occupied while their women shopped, and customers kept demanding more. Soon the restaurant required more help, and Tommy left his job of 25 years to become cook; later, more space was needed, and a covered deck joined two enclosed porches and an interior room as dining space.

Guarding her two remaining downstairs sales rooms, Linda displays merchandise all over the house, and posts the frequently-changing menu on blackboards. "It's just home cooking," she says. "A lot are my mother's recipes." Whatever you call it, food at Back Home is tasty.

The lunch crowd is primarily from nearby, enjoying chicken salad, sandwiches, and lighter entrées; most of the evening traffic is from out of town. Each night, they find eight vegetables—beets, cabbage, green beans, squash or broccoli casseroles—and five meats to choose from. Most popular is Roast Beef and Gravy, but Turkey and Dressing, Barbecued Spare Ribs, Pork Chops, and Meatloaf often appear.

Among desserts are creamy Chocolate Nut Pie, Cracker Dessert (a meringue-like confection with pecans and coconut) fruit cobblers, and their famous Praline Cheesecake.

Back Home, 251 West Dixie, Elizabethtown, is at the intersection of 31W and Miles Street, 1 block north of US 62. Lunch, Monday through Saturday, is 11 a.m. to 2 p.m.; dinner, Tuesday through Saturday, is 5 to 8 p.m. Gift shop is open Monday, 9 a.m. to 5 p.m., Tuesday through Saturday, 9 a.m. until 8 p.m. (502)769-2800. Dress is casual, reservations are not accepted, and the busiest time is during Christmas Open House, the first weekend in November. AE,MC,V. ($$)

BACK HOME CORN BREAD SALAD

12 corn muffins
1 cup chopped celery
1 cup chopped
  green peppers
1 cup chopped onion

1 cup mayonnaise
2 tomatoes, diced
Salt and pepper
Crumbled cooked bacon

In large bowl, crumble muffins, mix with vegetables and mayonnaise, then stir in tomatoes and seasonings. Sprinkle with crumbled bacon.

BACK HOME PINEAPPLE AU GRATIN

Two 20-ounce cans pine-
  apple chunks with juice
3/4 cup flour
2 cups shredded
  Cheddar cheese

1/2 cup sugar
1 tube Ritz™ crackers
4 ounces butter, melted

In large bowl, mix first 4 ingredients. Spread in baking pan or casserole, and crumble Ritz™ crackers on top. Drizzle melted butter over all, and bake at 350 degrees 45 minutes, or until lightly browned.

BACK HOME HOT FUDGE CAKE

1 cup flour
3/4 cup sugar
3 Tablespoons cocoa
1/2 cup milk
2 Tablespoons
  melted shortening

1 cup chopped pecans
1 cup brown sugar
2 cups hot water
Ice cream

In large bowl, mix first 3 ingredients; stir in next 3 ingredients, and spread in 9" x 13" pan. Sprinkle with brown sugar, then pour hot water over all. Bake at 350 degrees about 40 minutes. Serve warm, topped with ice cream.

BACK HOME
TOM'S DELICIOUS PEACH COBBLER

One 29-ounce can sliced
  peaches, with juice
3/4 cup water
1 cup sugar, divided

4 ounces butter
1 cup flour
1 cup milk

In saucepan, heat peaches, water, and 1/2 cup sugar to boiling; cook about 10 minutes. In 9" x 13" pan, melt butter in 350 degree oven. In bowl, mix flour, milk, and remaining sugar; pour into pan on top of melted butter. DO NOT MIX! Pour hot peach mixture on top of flour mixture and bake at 350 degrees 45 minutes or until brown. Bake covered 30 minutes, then uncovered 15 minutes.

THE WHISTLE STOP
RESTAURANT
Glendale

For generations, time has stood still in the quaint country village of Glendale. White houses starched with gingerbread sprawl in shady yards, neighbors wave as they go about their business, and the only disturbers of the peace are passing trains.

The station is gone now; trains are fewer and no longer stop, but the track still runs through town, and the flavor of the railroad years has been preserved in The Whistle Stop Restaurant.

In 1974, James and Idell Sego converted part of his track-side hardware store into a restaurant, incorporating ticket windows and other train station elements. Next door, a tumble-down log cabin was rebuilt as a cozy waiting room with a gift shop in the loft.

Soon visitors came from nearby Elizabethtown, and as word spread, travelers drove the two miles from I-65 for lunch, and groups planned day trips from Louisville and Bowling Green. Gift and antique shops moved to Glendale, which became THE place for an outing and a great meal. The village was placed on the National Register in 1988.

Expansion of The Whistle Stop eventually absorbed the entire hardware store. One narrow downstairs room has the feel of a dining car, with booths on each side; another has its own gabled roof; and a third is a country kitchen, complete with pump, wood stove, and cupboards filled with vintage implements.

Here, lunch might be a "Trainman Special" of creamed chicken on corn bread, or baked pork chops with potatoes and cream sauce; ladies love the tasty chicken salad with fruit salad and muffin. Popular dinners include pan-fried trout, salmon croquettes and stuffed pork chops, served with fresh country vegetables, salad, and homemade bread.

Upstairs, the Iron Horse Dining Room is a self-contained colonial tavern, where vegetables are passed at the table, and meals of fried chicken, country ham, and constantly changing "specials" are accompanied by soup, relish, and Idell's puffy little rolls.

The Whistle Stop's homemade desserts are outstanding. Sugar Cream Pie is meltingly sweet, with cinnamon; and chocolate, coconut and other pies and fruit cobblers have the same flaky light crusts; if you call ahead, you can take one home. Better yet, take two!

The Whistle Stop Restaurant, Main Street, Glendale, is about 5 miles southwest of Elizabethtown, 2 miles off I-65. It is open 11 a.m. to 9 p.m. Tuesday through Saturday, with a limited menu from 2 to 5 p.m. Dress is casual, and no reservations or credit cards are accepted; personal checks accepted. Derby Brunch is served 9 a.m. to 1 p.m., the first Saturday in May. ($$)

Reservations ARE accepted (but not required) in the Iron Horse Dining Room, where lunch is 11 a.m. to 1:30 p.m. and dinner 4:30 to 9 p.m., Tuesday through Saturday. ($$$) (502)369-8586.

WHISTLE STOP
ROAST PORK WITH APRICOT GLAZE

**4 to 5 pound
  pork loin roast
2 teaspoons salt
1/2 teaspoon pepper
3/4 cup (packed)
  brown sugar**

**2 1/2 teaspoons
  dry mustard
2 Tablespoons
  cornstarch
3 cups apricot nectar
4 teaspoons vinegar**

Rub roast well with salt and pepper and score fat. Insert meat thermometer into center (not touching bone or fat) place in open pan, and bake 35 minutes per pound at 325 degrees, until internal temperature reaches 170 degrees. In saucepan, mix brown sugar, mustard, and cornstarch. Stir in apricot nectar and vinegar, place over medium heat, and cook, stirring constantly, until thickened. About 1/2 hour before roast is done, glaze with 1/2 cup of sauce. Replace in oven until done. For easier carving, rest roast 20 minutes. Slice and serve with remaining glaze, mixed with 3 Tablespoons of brown drippings from roasting pan.

WHISTLE STOP
BRUSSELS SPROUTS AND CARROTS
WITH HOT BACON DRESSING

2 eggs
1/4 cup sugar
2/3 cup white vinegar
1/3 cup water
1/2 teaspoon dry mustard
1 teaspoon salt
1/3 teaspoon pepper

10 strips bacon,
   fried crisp and drained
Reserved bacon
   drippings
3-pound package frozen
   Brussels sprouts
10 or 12 ounce package
   baby carrots

In bowl, beat eggs lightly with a fork; add next 6 ingredients and blend. Over low heat, combine egg mixture with bacon drippings until thickened. Set aside. Cook sprouts and carrots in separate pots of salted boiling water. Do not overcook. Drain and combine gently; serve with warm sauce, garnished with crumbled bacon.

WHISTLE STOP CORN PUDDING

3 Tablespoons melted
   margarine
2 Tablespoons sugar
2 Tablespoons flour
1 teaspoon salt
3 large eggs

2 cups canned or frozen
   whole kernel corn
2 cups cream-style corn
1 1/2 cups
   half-and-half cream

In bowl, blend first four ingredients; beat in eggs. Stir in corn, then cream, blending well. Pour into greased 1 1/2 quart casserole and bake at 325 degrees 45 minutes, or until slightly puffed and golden brown.

MARIAH'S 1818
Bowling Green

As early as 1775, hunters explored an area near where the Cumberland Trace crossed the Barren River; McFadden's Station, built at the crossing about 1785, was an early fort and landmark for travelers. Robert Moore established himself at a nearby "big spring" in 1790, and in 1797 offered two acres for the construction of public buildings in new Warren County, named for General Joseph Warren, who fought at Bunker Hill.

Tradition says that court was held at the home of Robert and his brother George Moore until the construction of a courthouse, and that visitors often played a game of bowls on the lawn, giving the new town the name of Bowling Green.

George Moore and his wife Elizabeth built a Federal-style house at 801 State Street in 1818, at a cost of $4,000. It is believed to stand on the site of the Moore brothers' original home, and to be the oldest brick house in Bowling Green. George Moore died in 1819, but the house continued to be occupied by his widow, and his daughter Mariah lived there until her death in 1888.

Placed on the National Register in 1972, the house became a restaurant in 1980, named for Mariah Moore. It had changed little over the years, and the addition to the side of the building in 1990 was carefully designed to blend with the original structure. Adding a badly needed waiting area, it also contributed two new dining rooms, a bar, and outdoor seating on the roof, while lessening traffic in the older part.

Although long-removed walls both upstairs and down have altered the interior, the house still has some original floors, mantels, and woodwork; the large combination room upstairs sports a fireplace at each end and five big windows across the front.

The menu provides a wide selection, with vegetable, cheese, meat and poultry appetizers, spectacular salads (Sunny Florida Chicken Salad tops a mound of fresh fruit; its marmalade-honey dressing can't be beat!) hearty soups and sandwiches (the Crab Meat Asparagus Melt is a winner). Entrées of seafood, chicken, and pasta are always enticing, and Mariah's carefully selected beef provides great fillets, prime rib, and skewered steak in teriyaki sauce.

There's a different dessert of the day every day, and gooey concoctions such as Mariah's Delight (hot fudge,

161

pudding nut cake, ice cream and whipped cream) or Double Dare Delectable Delight (Oreo™ crust, frozen cheesecake, chocolate mousse, whipped cream, and Heath Bar™ chips) should satisfy the sweetest tooth.

Mariah's 1818, 801 State Street, Bowling Green, is open 11 a.m. to 10 p.m. Monday through Thursday, to 11 p.m. Friday and Saturday, and to 9 p.m. Sunday, with continuous service. (502)842-6878. All legal beverages are available, dress is casual, and reservations are requested for parties of 6 or more. AE,DC,MC,V. ($$)

MARIAH'S BROCCOLI CHEESE SOUP

1 bunch fresh broccoli	1 cup flour
1 quart milk	1 cup butter
1/2 pound	1/2 teaspoon salt
Velveeta Cheese™	1/2 teaspoon pepper

Cut florets from broccoli; place in saucepan and cover with water. Boil until just tender, drain, and chill. In saucepan, place sliced broccoli stalks covered with water, and boil until done. Purée stalks and remaining water in blender. In saucepan, heat milk over low heat; cut cheese into small pieces and add to hot milk, stirring until cheese is melted. Add purée and florets. Mix flour with butter until blended; drop by bits into broccoli mixture, and cook over medium heat until thickened, being careful not to boil. Season to taste. Serves 6.

MARIAH'S CALIFORNIA CHICKEN SALAD

2 pounds	4 Tablespoons sugar
boneless chicken	1/2 cup mayonnaise
1/4 cup seedless grapes,	3 Tablespoons
sliced	chopped parsley
1/3 cup chopped celery	Toasted almonds
Pinch salt	Fresh Fruit
Pinch white pepper	

Poach chicken breasts in water to cover until just done. Remove from liquid, cool, and dice small. Add remaining ingredients. Serve with toasted almonds and fresh fruit. Serves 5.

MARIAH'S APPLESAUCE MUFFINS

1 cup softened butter	2 teaspoons baking soda
2 cups sugar	1 Tablespoon cinnamon
2 eggs	2 teaspoons allspice
3 teaspoons vanilla	1 teaspoon cloves
4 cups flour	2 cups applesauce

In large bowl, combine first 4 ingredients and mix well. In another bowl, combine dry ingredients. Add to butter mixture and stir; mix in applesauce thoroughly. Spoon batter into greased muffin tin (or use paper liners) and bake at 350 degrees 20 to 25 minutes until of cake-like texture and slightly browned. Cool in pan on rack.

MARIAH'S 1818 CHEESECAKE

2 cups graham cracker crumbs	1 1/2 cups sugar
1/4 cup sugar	4 eggs
1/4 cup melted butter	2 teaspoons vanilla
Three 8-ounce packages cream cheese	1 Tablespoon lemon juice

Mix first 3 ingredients and press into bottom of 8" springform pan. In large bowl of mixer, cream cheese and sugar at high speed; reduce speed to low and add eggs one at a time, then add vanilla and lemon juice and mix thoroughly. Pour onto crust and bake at 350 degrees 1 hour, until golden brown around the edges. (Center may still be soft.) Cool on wire rack. Run a knife around edge of pan and release sides of pan.

THE PARAKEET CAFÉ
Bowling Green

In the mid-nineteenth century, as the importance of railroads became evident, there was much competition among cities in south-central Kentucky to be on the route of the Louisville and Nashville Railroad. Bowling Green was successful, and the line to Nashville opened in 1859. Trade was brisk between the two cities until the War Between the States closed the railroad in Tennessee, cutting off Bowling Green from the South.

On September 18, 1861, the Commonwealth of Kentucky, previously holding to a position of neutrality, declared itself for the Union; on that same day, Confederate forces invaded Bowling Green. For five months, the city was occupied by 25,000 Confederate troops, and served as headquarters of the Confederate Army of the West, under the command of General Albert Sidney Johnston, a Kentuckian.

Several fortifications built by the Confederates on hills surrounding Bowling Green were later captured and improved by Union forces; portions of three still exist, and have been placed on the National Register of Historic Places.

Just a block from Fountain Square, a little building of obscure origins has existed quietly for generations, serving as livery stable, blacksmith shop, laundry, and delicatessen, and used at one time for storage of caskets for a funeral home.

Since 1975, it has been the Parakeet Café, with food as clever and bright as its decor. Who would believe this unprepossessing structure could be so open and airy? Ceiling joists have been removed, leaving stout chains to hold exposed-brick walls together, and creating a bistro effect that is at once intimate and friendly. A mezzanine and a side addition are used for seating, as well as the main room; there is much laughter and exchange between tables, and no one minds waiting for a seat—this is one of the area's most popular eateries.

Owner Lon Durbin was an employee when the Parakeet was new; after experience in several other fine restaurants, he and a partner purchased it in 1983. Sole owner since early 1991, he describes the Parakeet's cuisine as "Western Kentucky food with a California twist." That means fresh, locally produced foods, imaginatively combined into creations such as Black-eyed Pea Fritters, Barbecue Pie (Kentucky smoked pork in barbecue sauce as filling of a miniature two-crust pie), and Kentucky Carbonara (country ham, bacon, and scallions in cream, over fettuccine).

Lon's stay in New Orleans is responsible for Jambalaya, Veal Prudhomme, and some of the best Rémoulade sauce you'll ever taste; a recent fascination with "Grandmother's recipes" has produced entrées of Chicken Fried Steak, Open-faced Hot Roast Beef Sandwich, and Meatloaf, served with REAL mashed potatoes and home-cooked vegetables.

Nightly specials reflect new ideas and "whatever's fresh," and favorite desserts include Mokoko Cheesecake, Crème Caramel, Marci's Butterscotch Pecan Pie, and a dense homemade fudge brownie topped with ice cream.

The Parakeet Café, 951 Chestnut Street, Bowling Green, is in the middle of Chestnut Street, between Main and 10th, and is open 11 a.m. to 10 p.m., Monday through Thursday, until 11 p.m. Friday, and 5 to 11 p.m. Saturday. (502)781-1538. Dress is "tennis to tuxedo", all legal beverages are available, with many wines by the glass, and reservations are accepted for parties of 6 or more. AE,MC,V, personal checks. ($$)

THE PARAKEET CAFÉ
GRILLED CHICKEN SALAD

For each serving:
6-ounce chicken
  breast half
1/2 cup vinaigrette
  salad dressing
1/2 sweet pepper,
  sliced thin
6 to 10 small fresh
  asparagus spears,

  lightly steamed
Mixed garden greens
1 ounce feta cheese
6 to 10 ripe olives
5 rings thinly
  sliced purple onion
Additional dressing

Marinate chicken in dressing 1 hour; grill or broil until done. Slice into 1/4" to 1/2" strips. Fan strips alternately with peppers and asparagus on greens. Crumble cheese over salad, top with olives and onions, and serve with additional dressing.

THE PARAKEET CAFÉ CHICKEN MILANO WITH TOMATO BASIL CREAM

2 cups fresh
  bread crumbs
1/2 cup Parmesan cheese
1/2 Tablespoon salt
1/4 cup chopped
  fresh parsley
1/4 cup chopped
  fresh basil
8 ounces butter, melted

2 cloves garlic, minced
2 Tablespoons
  Dijon mustard
1 Tablespoon
  Worcestershire sauce
6 boneless, skinless
  chicken breast halves
Pasta (your choice)
  cooked al denté
Tomato Basil Cream

Mix first 5 ingredients; set aside in shallow pan. Mix next 4 ingredients; dip breasts in this mixture, then coat with dry mixture. Bake at 350 degrees 20 to 25 minutes. Serve with pasta, tossed with Tomato Basil Cream. Serves 6.

For Tomato Basil Cream: Into non-reactive pan, pour 1 pint heavy cream, bring to boil, and reduce by half. Add 3/8 cup chopped fresh basil, 1/2 teaspoon pepper, 1/2 teaspoon salt, and 4 cups tomato sauce, and simmer 5 minutes. Yields about 5 cups sauce.

THE PARAKEET CAFÉ ANN'S PEPPER RELISH

4 cups chopped
  red sweet peppers
2 cups chopped
  green peppers
2 cups chopped onion

1/2 cup chopped
  hot banana peppers
3/4 cup sugar
1 cup vinegar
1 Tablespoon salt

In non-reactive pan, place all vegetables , cover with water, and boil 2 minutes. Drain water from vegetables, add remaining ingredients, and simmer 45 minutes.

WOODBURY HOUSE
Woodbury

The Green River was first used for transportation by native Americans; archaeological exploration has located hundreds of encampments along its banks. In 1778, dispossessed settlers from Boonesboro relocated to lands at the mouth of the Green River, and flatboat trade developed from the interior down the Green, Ohio, and Mississippi rivers.

In 1828, the river was surveyed from Evansville, Indiana, to Bowling Green, and the state authorized locks and dams on the Green and Barren rivers, the first slackwater canalization project built in the United States. Completed in 1842, the project totaled 175 river miles, prompting regularly scheduled steamboat traffic that lasted over 100 years.

In 1886, Kentucky ceded its rights along the river to the United States; Congress appropriated monies, and in 1888, the U. S. took possession of the river and began construction of government buildings at Lock and Dam Number Four at Woodbury.

At the site were a house for the superintendent, an office building, shipyards, warehouses, a dry dock, a dredging fleet, a railroad system, and a crew of nearly eighty people; this was headquarters for all river operations on the Green, Barren, Rough, Mud, and Nolin rivers.

Some operations were shifted to Paducah and Louisville in the 1930s and 1940s, but the center remained in operation until 1973, despite a break in the dam in 1965. The property was deeded to Butler County in 1975, and was placed on the National Register in 1980.

Work on the Corps of Engineers Workmen's Office Building probably began in 1889 so it could be used during construction. This deceptively small-looking story-and-a-half structure has yellow brick walls in a Flemish bond pattern, with headers of a burnt orange color. Sheltered by a broad porch, it resembles the Superintendent's house (now a museum) nearby, and has a comfortable homey feeling, whether you're enjoying the view from the porch, or fine Kentucky food in the pleasant dining rooms.

Woodbury House, a restaurant since 1985, has been under the management of Betty and Don Locke since October of 1990. Its "Happy food" is like the best memories of childhood meals at an older relative's home—tasty food, a bit fancier than everyday, and plenty of everything.

Each meal provides an appetizer, a choice of either fried chicken, country ham, or another meat that might be Chicken Supreme (boneless breast with bacon/sour cream/mushroom sauce), Oven Roasted Sirloin of Beef, or Cider-Baked Ham. Serving bowls on each table contain four or five vegetables (always superb Summer Slaw), possibly "cut-off" corn, buttered parsley potatoes, glazed carrots with pineapple, green limas, or fried green apples. Also included are beverage, bread, and a choice of delicious homemade desserts.

There's always pecan pie and cheesecake, and from time to time, apple pie or cobbler, Italian Cream Cake, Sour Cream Cake with fresh fruit, or Betty's Cool Cake, with pineapple-orange filling. If you're really lucky, you might be there on a day when there's fresh, locally picked, blackberry cobbler with perfect flaky crust and ice cream on top.

Woodbury House is on Woodbury Loop, just off KY 263 at the Green River and 25 minutes north of I-65; from Green River Parkway, exit at Morgantown and follow KY 231 into Morgantown, then KY 403 about 4 miles to Woodbury—watch for signs. The restaurant is open Friday and Saturday nights for "supper" from 5:30 to 8:30, and for Sunday dinner from 12 noon until 2:30 p.m. (502) 526-6921. Dress is casual, and reservations are VERY important; busiest time is during December. MC,V, Personal checks. ($)

WOODBURY HOUSE SUMMER SLAW

6 cups coarsely
  shredded cabbage
2 tomatoes, chopped
1 large green pepper,
  chopped

1/2 teaspoon salt
1/2 cup Miracle Whip™
  salad dressing
2 Tablespoons sugar

In large bowl, gently combine all ingredients.

WOODBURY HOUSE BEAN SOUP

2 pounds white beans
1 cup finely grated
  carrots

1 onion, chopped fine
1 meaty ham hock
1 Tablespoon salt

In large, deep pot, place first 4 ingredients; cover generously with cold water, and cook over medium heat about 2 hours.

Add salt, and cook 1 hour, or until beans are tender, adding water if necessary. Mash some of the beans to make a good, thick, soup. Correct seasoning.

WOODBURY HOUSE CHICKEN VINEYARD

8 chicken breast halves
Salt and pepper
Flour for dredging
4 ounces butter
1 large onion,
   cut into rings

4 strips raw bacon,
   chopped
1/3 cup cooking sherry

Salt and pepper chicken; roll in flour. In skillet, melt butter and BROWN chicken, but do not cook. Remove breasts to casserole and top with onion and bacon. With sherry, rinse remaining butter from skillet and pour over chicken. Cover and bake at 350 degrees 1 hour or until fork-tender. Serve on a bed of rice. Serves 8.

WOODBURY HOUSE "TWICE-BAKED" CHEESECAKE

Baked graham
   cracker crust
Three 8-ounce packages
   cream cheese

1 1/4 cups sugar, divided
4 eggs
1 teaspoon vanilla
16 ounces sour cream

In large bowl of mixer, blend cream cheese with 3/4 cup sugar; add eggs one at a time, then vanilla. Pour into crust and bake 45 to 50 minutes at 350 degrees. Blend sour cream with remaining sugar. Open oven, spread on cheesecake, and bake 10 minutes at 350 degrees. Serves 12.

For crust: mix 1 cup crushed graham crackers with 1/3 cup sugar. Add 6 Tablespoons melted butter. Press on bottom of 9" or 10" springform pan; grease sides of pan.

COLBY'S
Owensboro

Daviess County was named for Major Joseph Hamilton Daveiss (the spelling was changed), who was born in Virginia in 1774. After military service, he studied law and entered the office of George Nicholas in Lexington, becoming United States Attorney for Kentucky. In 1801, he was the first "western" lawyer to appear before the Supreme Court; he made his home at "Cornland" on the outskirts of what is now Owensboro.

A strong admirer of Alexander Hamilton, Daveiss took Hamilton's surname as his own middle name; he hated former Vice President Aaron Burr, who killed Hamilton in a duel. In 1806, at Frankfort, Daveiss brought an indictment against Burr who planned, among other things, to attack Mexico and to separate western lands from the United States. Although he accepted money from both Britain and Spain for traitorous purposes, Burr had many powerful friends in Kentucky, including Henry Clay. He was found not guilty at both his trials, but fled to Europe to escape public opinion.

Daveiss rejoined the army in 1811, and was killed leading a charge of Kentuckians at the battle of Tippecanoe. He is remembered as a man of intelligence, judgment, and courage.

When Daviess County was formed in 1815, its county seat was laid out at a little settlement on the Ohio River known as "Yellow Banks" by flatboat men. It was first settled in 1797 by William Smeathers (also given as Smothers and Smithers) who served in the Kentucky Militia and the War of 1812.

Strategically located on the Ohio, Owensboro became a trading center for a large and rich agricultural region. It rapidly developed an industrial economy as well, and its handsome downtown area reflects the prosperity that prevailed around the end of the nineteenth century.

Just a few yards from Smeathers cabin site, the Odd Fellows Building was constructed at St. Ann and Third streets in 1895. A three-story commercial building of yellow brick, it incorporates elements of several styles of architecture, and houses professional offices and the lodge hall at upper levels. It was placed on the National Register in 1986, and since 1987, the first floor has housed Colby's restaurant, known for "fine food and spirits."

In an airy, open atmosphere, with high ceilings, tile floors and exposed-brick walls showcasing local art works, Colby's version of American Cuisine is light and flavorful. The emphasis is on Louisiana foods—Cajun Chicken, New Orleans Gumbo, and a different Muffaletta sandwich—but you'll find a variety of burgers, hearty sandwiches, and a generous assortment of salads and appetizers.

Entrées include ribs, prime or barbecued; pastas; and excellent chicken dishes—the House Chicken is a charbroiled breast with smoked ham and Monterey jack cheese in a spicy sauce—and always a charbroiled or pan-blackened fresh fish.

Specialty drinks such as Peaches and Cream (peaches, peach brandy, and French vanilla ice cream whirled to milkshake consistency) might tempt you, but check out Colby's tasty desserts. Toll House® Pie, Fudge Nut Brownie and deep dish Apple Walnut Pie are served with ice cream, and Colby's makes REAL milkshakes, just for the kid in you.

Colby's, 202 West Third Street, Owensboro, is open 11 a.m. to 11 p.m., Monday through Thursday, until 12 midnight Friday and Saturday. (502)685-4239. All legal beverages are available, plus many wines by the glass; dress is casual, and reservations are accepted only for parties of 6 or more. AE,MC,V. ($$)

COLBY'S ORANGE DRESSING

1/2 cup orange juice   **1/4 cup honey**
1 cup heavy cream   **1/4 cup apricot preserves**

In bowl, combine all ingredients and mix. Pour into container of blender and process 20 seconds on low. Yields about 2 cups.

Note: this is the dressing served on Colby's Chicken Fruit Salad; it is suggested for use with any fresh fruit.

COLBY'S CHICKEN AND RICE SOUP

4 quarts water
1/2 cup chicken base OR
  very strong chicken
  stock
1 1/2 pounds boneless,
  skinless chicken breast
  in 3/4" cubes
1/2 cup diced celery
1/2 cup diced red onion
1/2 cup diced carrot
1/2 green pepper, diced
1 1/2 teaspoons oregano
1 1/2 teaspoons
  white pepper
1 1/2 teaspoons salt
1 1/2 teaspoons
  yellow food coloring
6 cups PRECOOKED
  white rice

In large stockpot, heat water and stock to boil. Add chicken and vegetables and cook on medium heat until chicken is done, about 15 minutes. Add spices and coloring, return to boil, and cook 5 minutes more, stirring often. Add rice and heat through. Yields about 25 servings.

COLBY'S TOLL HOUSE® PIE

One 9-inch
  unbaked pie shell
4 eggs
3/4 cup (packed) brown
  sugar
3/4 cup sugar
1 cup flour
8 ounces softened
  butter
1 1/4 cups
  chopped walnuts
1 1/4 cups chocolate
  chips

In large bowl, beat eggs until foamy; add sugars, then flour, and stir until well blended. Fold in butter, then add walnuts and chips. Pour into pie shell and bake at 325 degrees for 1 hour.

Note: best if cooled and refrigerated before cutting. If reheated in microwave, heat no longer than 30 seconds.

TROTTERS
Owensboro

Tobacco was used by Native Americans for ritual, medicinal, and social purposes, possibly as early as 3000 B.C. Its smoke, a general purifier, also cured respiratory and gastric problems; tobacco was taken internally as a purgative and remedy for parasites, and occasionally as a hallucinogen; and it was applied externally as a disinfectant and poultice.

When Europeans arrived, they learned the uses and cultivation of tobacco, and took it back to their countries, starting a rage for tobacco that spread to all continents, making it the most widely used addictive drug in the world.

Early settlers began to cultivate tobacco commercially almost as soon as they arrived in Virginia in 1607. A century and a half later, pioneers in Kentucky continued the practice, but primarily for local trade—shipping half-ton hogsheads of tobacco across the Appalachians was nearly impossible. Downriver shipment to New Orleans for European trade was also risky, due to low water on the Kentucky River, Indians, river pirates, and Spanish officials at the port city.

James Wilkinson, founder of Frankfort, negotiated traitorously with Louisiana Spanish in 1787, and built a thriving trade in tobacco and other Kentucky produce. His charges were high, and by the 1790s, farmers were forming flatboat convoys from Louisville to New Orleans.

Regular steamboat traffic on the Ohio in the 1820s encouraged tobacco production in the western part of the state, where navigable rivers were natural routes to shipping centers; river towns not only warehoused tobacco, but built factories to process it.

A seven-story warehouse built in Owensboro in 1892 by the American Tobacco Company was the largest wooden building in the world; it was reduced to two (brick) stories in 1956, when it became a "Roi-Tan" cigar factory, producing 665 million ten-cent cigars in 1965. By 1976, it was the only cigar factory in Kentucky; it closed in 1978, and was converted to a retail and office mall in the early 1980s.

Today, it houses an outpatient surgical center, a mortgage firm, professional offices, and Trotters Restaurant, a "fun" eatery with a trotting-track theme. Dining alcoves are set apart by brass rails that mimic horse stalls, and exposed brick walls and natural woods create a relaxed, comfortable atmosphere in which light or traditional meals may be enjoyed.

Chef John Brett bought management experience and classical chef training to the restaurant he bought in 1988. His menu is made up of items first tried as house specials— when they proved popular, they were kept.

Appetizers (sautéed shrimp and crab baked in a pastry shell, artichokes stuffed with cream cheese) and salads (chargrilled tuna Provençal, grilled sirloin on greens) are creative and unusual; burgers and sandwiches (chargrilled salmon fillet with cream cheese on a bagel) are hearty and tasty; and dinners of roasted prime rib, Chicken Santa Fe (marinated breast with salsa, avocado, and melted cheese) and Steak and Shrimp Brochettes are generously served.

At Trotters, regional foods are stressed, and everything possible is prepared to order. Meals begin with a hot croissant drizzled with honey butter, and might end with Oreo™ Cookies-and-Cheese Cheesecake, Lemon Meringue Pie, or Strawberry Trifle—pound cake, ice cream, fresh berries, sherry, almonds, etc., etc. You'll love it.

Trotters, 1100 Walnut Street, Owensboro, is open 11 a.m. to 10 p.m., Monday through Thursday, to 11 p.m. Friday and Saturday. (502)685-2771. All legal beverages are available, dress is casual, and reservations are accepted only for parties of 5 or more. AE,MC,V. ($$)

TROTTERS STUFFED ARTICHOKE HEARTS PHILADELPHIA

For each serving: **Buttermilk for dipping**
5 canned **Self-rising flour**
  artichoke hearts **Oil for frying**
Cream cheese stuffing

Using cocktail fork, remove center from artichokes. Fill center with stuffing. Dip artichokes in buttermilk and dredge in flour, packing flour tight. In wok or deep fryer, fry artichokes in oil until golden brown. Serve with honey-mustard dressing.

For cream cheese stuffing: blend 8 ounces cream cheese with 2 ounces Dijon mustard; should yield 2 servings.

TROTTERS GRILLED SHRIMP
AND SPINACH SALAD

For each serving:
5 very large raw shrimp
2 ounces Italian dressing
3 cups spinach leaves,
  washed and stemmed
1 1/2 ounces mushrooms,
  in 1/4" slices

Bacon bits
3 rings red onion
1 tomato, quartered
1 hard-cooked egg,
  quartered

Marinate shrimp in dressing 1/2 hour. Mound spinach on chilled salad plate; top with mushrooms, bacon bits, and onion rings. Alternate wedges of tomato and egg around plate. Grill shrimp about 2 minutes per side; arrange on top of salad. Serve with Hot Bacon Dressing.

TROTTERS HOT BACON DRESSING

1/4 pound raw bacon,
  in 1/4" dice
1/4 pound yellow onion,
  diced
1/4 cup flour

1/4 pound chicken base*
1 cup hot water*
1 cup cider vinegar
1 cup sugar
Pinch cayenne pepper

In saucepan, sauté bacon until firm. Add onion and cook until transparent. Stir in flour and cook about 1 1/2 minutes. Dissolve chicken base* in hot water and vinegar; stir into bacon mixture and cook over medium heat until thickened, adding sugar and cayenne while stirring. May be refrigerated and reheated when needed. Yields about 3 cups.

*Chicken base is a commercial product not readily available to the consumer; 1 cup very strong chicken stock may be substituted for the hot water and chicken base.

WOLF'S TAVERN
Henderson

Oone of the most colorful people in early Kentucky history was Richard Henderson: lawyer, judge, land speculator, and visionary. Henderson was organizer and chief promoter of The Transylvania Company, which, in 1775, bought the land between the Cumberland, Kentucky, and Ohio rivers from the Cherokee Indians, and sent Daniel Boone to open up the Wilderness Trail.

When the transaction was declared void by Virginia in 1778, the Transylvania Company was compensated for its loss of the settlement at Boonesboro by a grant of two hundred thousand acres on the Ohio at the mouth of the Green River. Most of the company settled in the area and prospered; Henderson remained in North Carolina, but the county and its seat are named for him.

Henderson's most famous resident was wildlife artist/ naturalist John J. Audubon, who was born in Santo Domingo and grew up in France. Sent to Philadelphia to manage family property, he married and came west with his bride, traveling down the Ohio River to Louisville, then Henderson. Some of his best known pictures were painted in the area, where he lived from 1810 to 1819. Audubon State Park, just outside Henderson, contains a nature preserve and a museum devoted to his work.

The rich land that supported wildlife provided a good living for people, also; Henderson became an agricultural community, with tobacco the chief product. In 1835, there were 15 tobacco stemmeries, employing 1,000 people of a population of 8,000; by 1870, the population had increased to over 18,000, and Henderson produced more tobacco than any other county in Kentucky.

In 1878, George Wolf, a young German immigrant, built a two-story brick bakery on the corner of Green and First streets; he married a local girl named Augusta, and they lived, with their eight children, in the adjacent residence. About 1903, the business became a tavern, receiving the state's second (after Talbott's) package liquor permit—and drink license number nine.

Reduced to a candy store during prohibition, Wolf's was again a tavern during the depression, when it survived by adding bean soup and chili to homemade bread and cheese for its first, limited menu. Known as the place "Where Friends Meet," the restaurant/tavern remained in Wolf's family for three generations, until his granddaughter retired in 1981.

Brief occupancy in the mid-1980s was followed by two years of vacancy, but Wolf's re-opened in 1987 after a renovation that restored much of its early appearance. The striking metal cornice pediment, the only one of its type remaining in the area, still proclaims "G. Wolf" on the roof and as the tavern's logo, and terrific bean soup is still served daily in a friendly, convivial atmosphere. As part of the Henderson Commercial District, Wolf's Tavern was placed on the National Register in 1989.

There's always something going on at Wolf's; friends STILL meet to lunch on a "Wolfburger" (a five-ounce chuck burger charbroiled to order), the popular Kentucky Hot Brown sandwich, or Greek or chicken salad. On "special" evenings, they look forward to spaghetti on Monday, catfish fiddler fillets on Friday, and Prime Rib on Saturday, with other choices such as shrimp scampi, fried chicken livers, Chicken Cordon Bleu, and Three-Way Pork Chops, followed by creamy White Chocolate/Raspberry Swirl Cheesecake, or Turtle Cheesecake, and hearty winter peach and cherry cobblers.

And on the "fun" holidays (St. Patrick's Day, Halloween, Valentine's Day, etc.) there are week-long celebrations that may include music, appropriate foods, or special guests to ensure your enjoyment and swift return to "Where Friends Meet."

Wolf's Tavern, 31 North Green Street, on the corner of First, is entered from the side. It is open 6 days a week, and food is offered from 11 a.m. to 9 p.m., Monday through Thursday, until 10 p.m. Friday and Saturday. Bean soup is available even when kitchen is closed. (502)826-5221. All legal beverages are available, dress is casual, and reservations are accepted. AE,MC,V. ($$)

WOLF'S TAVERN BEAN SOUP

7 cups water	1 small onion, chopped
1 pound dried	1/2 teaspoon salt
Northern white beans	Dash of garlic pepper
2 cups chopped ham	10 3/4-ounce can
2 Tablespoons	tomato soup
bacon seasoning	

In large pot, combine all ingredients. Cover and simmer 11/4 hours, or until beans are tender. Add water during cooking if necessary. Serves 7.

WOLF'S TAVERN CHICKEN WALNUT SALAD

2 cups white
  chicken meat, cubed
1 cup chopped celery
1/2 cup walnuts
1/2 cup salad dressing
  (mayonnaise type)

2 Tablespoons
  corn syrup
1 teaspoon salt
1/4 teaspoon pepper
2-ounce jar sliced
  pimientos, drained

In large bowl, mix all ingredients; refrigerate until chilled, at least 1 1/2 hours.

WOLF'S TAVERN
MARINATA GRILLED CHICKEN

6 boned chicken breast
  halves
1/2 cup margarine or
  butter
1/4 cup vegetable oil
2 Tablespoons
  lemon juice

2 teaspoons salt
2 teaspoons sugar
1/2 teaspoon paprika
1/2 teaspoon
  ground ginger
1 teaspoon
  chopped garlic

Place chicken breasts on grill. In saucepan, combine remaining ingredients and heat, stirring occasionally, until margarine is melted. Brush on chicken every 10 minutes, turning chicken as it browns. Grill 15 to 20 minutes, or until done. Serves 6.

WOLF'S TAVERN COLADA

1 ounce rum
1 1/2 ounces Irish
  Cream™ liqueur

2 teaspoons coconut milk
2 ounces pineapple juice
2 cups crushed ice

Place all ingredients in electric blender; blend at high speed. Pour into soda glass and serve with a short straw.

BARTHOLOMEW'S
Hopkinsville

In 1796, a North Carolinian named Bartholomew Wood ended his search for land in the western part of Kentucky, and erected a log cabin near The Rock Spring, a landmark not far from the crossing of the Russellville trail and the Little River.

In this fertile Pennyroyal (pronounced, and often spelled, "Pennyrile") region of Kentucky, changes came fast. Within the next year, a new county was established, named for Patrick Henry's brother-in-law, Colonel William Christian, a Revolutionary War hero killed by Indians while attempting to settle the area that is now Louisville.

The Christian County seat was to be between the forks of Little River at The Rock Spring, and Bartholomew Wood donated five acres of land for the public buildings. The town that grew up around this center, originally named Elizabeth, was renamed for General Samuel Hopkins in 1804.

Wood is commemorated by two monuments: a statue in Hopkinsville's pioneer cemetery, and a restaurant on the site of his original cabin.

There is little of the pioneer spirit in Bartholomew's, however; the building it occupies, a brick, terra cotta and stone structure of Romanesque architecture, was built in 1894 as The Racket Store, which sold buggies and general merchandise. The structure, later used by hardware stores and an auto parts store, was placed on the National Register in 1979.

In 1982, a sensitive restoration adapted the lower portion as the dining room, and the mezzanine, left from a 1920s remodeling, as the bar; upper floors are used for office space and a banquet room. The open, airy restaurant is filled with plants, light, and interesting photographs of Hopkinsville's past. There's even a picture of Bartholomew T. Wood, son of the founder, and a copy of the original deed to the property.

Bartholomew's approach to food emphasizes quality, presentation, and service, and features fresh ingredients in unusual combinations. Entrées such as Chicken Alfredo, Beef Kabobs, and Mandarin Pork Chops are interestingly prepared and generously served; salads—Crazy Ann's, with chili and cheese, and Chicken-Pineapple, with fresh fruit and orange-apricot sauce—are accompanied by freshly baked croissants drizzled with honey butter, and burgers and sandwiches are piled high with extras.

If you still have room, don't miss Bartholomew's Toll House® Pie, served warm, oozing melted chocolate chips, and topped with vanilla ice cream.

Bartholomew's, 914 South Main Street, Hopkinsville, is on the corner of 10th Street. Lunch, Monday through Friday, is 11 a.m. to 2:30 p.m. Dinner, Monday through Thursday, is 5 to 9:30 p.m., Friday until 11 p.m. Saturday hours are 11 a.m. to 11 p.m., with continuous service that includes brunch, lunch, and dinner. (502)886-5768. Dress is casual, all legal beverages are served, and reservations are not accepted; call ahead for preferred seating. AE,MC,V. ($$)

BARTHOLOMEW'S SHRIMP LOUISIANE

6 Tablespoons butter
3 Tablespoons Paul
  Prudhomme's
  Cajun Magic™

6 large shrimp, deveined
  and peeled, tails on
  French or sourdough
  bread

In cast iron skillet, heat butter and Cajun Magic™ until hot; add shrimp and cook until pink and done. Serve in skillet with bread to soak up spicy butter.

BARTHOLOMEW'S PLANTATION CHICKEN

For each serving:
One 6-ounce boneless
  chicken breast
2 Tablespoons
  melted butter
Seasoning salt to taste

1/3 cup each of
  several vegetables
Bottled barbecue sauce
2 strips cooked bacon
Monterey jack cheese

Sauté first 3 ingredients in cast iron skillet over medium heat. Remove chicken and keep warm; sauté vegetables (squash, celery, sweet peppers, etc.)until hot but still crisp. Place chicken on warmed plate; top with barbecue sauce, then vegetables and bacon. Cover with cheese and place under broiler to melt.

BARTHOLOMEW'S CHICKEN SANTE FE

For each serving:
One boneless chicken
breast
Bottled barbecue
sauce

Black bean relish
2 strips cooked bacon
Monterey jack cheese
Sour cream

Grill chicken until done. Top with barbecue sauce, black bean relish, bacon, and cheese. Place under broiler to melt and finish with a dollop of sour cream.

For black bean relish: mix 1/4 cup each cooked and drained black beans, chopped tomato, sweet red pepper, sweet green pepper, and jalapeño pepper. Add 1 teaspoon lime juice, 2 teaspoons vegetable oil and 1 teaspoon granulated garlic.

BARTHOLOMEW'S
STRAWBERRY SHORTCAKE (drink)

3 scoops vanilla
ice cream
2 ounces
crushed strawberries
1/2 ounce amaretto

1/2 ounce
strawberry liqueur
Whipped cream
One perfect strawberry

In blender, blend first four ingredients. Pour into large glass; top with whipped cream and strawberry.

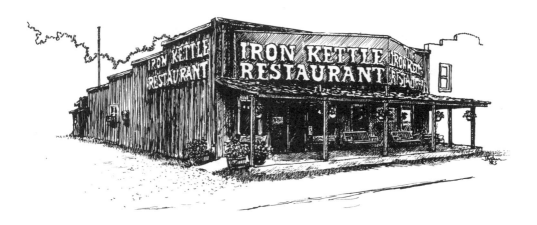

THE IRON KETTLE
Grand Rivers

When Thomas Lawson, a Boston businessman and promoter, came to the land between the Tennessee and Cumberland rivers in the mid-1870s, it was an area of ironworks. Oxen hauled wood to be burned for charcoal needed by the furnaces; ore was transported by wagonloads and pig iron was shipped on the rivers.

Excited by the thriving industry and a new railroad, Lawson and his backers founded the new town of Grand Rivers, and built another furnace, handsome houses, and a business section called "The Boston Block." Incorporating an entire city block of stores and offices and a hotel, it was an important part of the town that was intended to rival Pittsburgh.

Local ore was inferior, however, and more easily mined ore discovered in northern Alabama doomed the local industry. Lawson left quietly one night in 1918, abandoning his project, and unemployed ironworkers found work in the burgeoning gravel business.

Each time that misfortune came to Grand Rivers, better times followed; even the disastrous 1937 flood ultimately resulted in the two lakes that now provide tourism for the entire area. Kentucky Lake, Lake Barkley and The Land Between the Lakes attract thousands of people each year for fishing and recreation in scenic waters and unspoiled woodland.

Although much of The Boston Block was burned in 1940, the City Hall, at one end, and The Iron Kettle restaurant, at the other, have rebuilt. Hungry fisherfolk know The Iron Kettle as the home of "real country cooking," provided for 22 years by Mabel Nash and a hardworking crew.

People from every country in the world, as many as a thousand a day on summer weekends, have served themselves repeatedly with The Iron Kettle's bounty. Those unfamiliar with such regional foods as hominy, pea salad, and chicken gizzard stew have been surprised and pleased, have taken "just a little more," then have brought their friends.

Two old-fashioned wood stoves, now heated by gas, serve as buffets, with homemade yeast and corn breads in the ovens and choices of meats and vegetables on top. On a typical day, chicken and dumplings, ham and beans, and fried chicken are accompanied by broccoli casserole, baked beans, baked apples, turnip greens, butter beans, and stewed tomatoes, with a 50-item salad bar and peach and apple cobbler for dessert. Homemade bread is available to take out, if you're still hungry.

There is fried fish evenings and weekends, seafood on Friday nights, and hearty breakfasts to order in the mornings. This is the place to bring a real outdoors appetite!

The Iron Kettle, Grand Rivers, is open from about the first of March until the Sunday before Thanksgiving (depending upon weather) from 6 a.m. to 8:30 p.m., 7 days a week. (502)362-8396. Grand Rivers is between Lakes Barkley and Kentucky, off I-24 at exit 31, to KY 453 S, about 3 miles. Dress is casual; reservations are necessary only for large parties; personal checks are accepted; no credit cards. ($)

IRON KETTLE SWEET POTATO CASSEROLE

1/2 cup melted butter	1/2 cup pecans
1 cup brown sugar	3 cups cooked, mashed
1/2 cup flour	sweet potatoes

Mix all these ingredients together.

1 cup sugar	1/2 cup milk
2 eggs, beaten	1 Tablespoon vanilla
1/2 cup melted butter	

Mix all these ingredients together. Combine both groups of ingredients, pour into greased pan, and bake at 350 degrees 30 minutes. Serves 4 to 6.

IRON KETTLE KENTUCKY STYLE
HOT GERMAN POTATO SALAD

2 tablespoons pimientos
1 cup chopped celery
1 cup chopped
  sweet green peppers
1 cup chopped onion
1 teaspoon
  whole celery seed

1 cup vinegar
1 Tablespoon salt
1 cup sugar
Two 16-ounce cans sliced
  potatoes, drained
Polish sausage or
  wieners, cooked

In saucepan, place first five ingredients and mix with vinegar, salt, and sugar. Cook until celery is tender. Add potatoes and sausage or wieners just before serving. Serves 4 to 6.

IRON KETTLE KRAUT CASSEROLE

4 ounces butter
  (no substitute)
16-ounce can
  whole tomatoes,
  crushed
1 cup chopped onion

16-ounce can
  chopped sauerkraut
1 1/2 cups sugar
1 Tablespoon cornstarch
Crumbled cooked bacon
Grated cheese

In large saucepan, melt butter; add tomatoes, onion, and kraut and boil until onion is tender. Stir in sugar and cornstarch and pour into greased baking pan. Sprinkle bacon on top, then cheese. Bake until cheese is melted. Serves 4 to 6.

THE NINTH STREET HOUSE
Paducah

In 1795, for service during the Revolution, General George Rogers Clark was awarded substantial acreage in what is now southwestern Kentucky. He willed a tract at the confluence of the Ohio and Tennessee rivers to his brother, General William Clark, noted for his exploration of the West with Meriwether Lewis. Clark renamed the existing village of Pekin for friendly Indian Chief Paduke, and laid out the streets of a larger town on the site. Paducah's early success was tied to river traffic, and the town grew as an industrial and commercial center.

A great-nephew of the Clarks, George Wallace, built his winter home in Paducah's "Lower Town" in 1886. The large Queen Anne-style house was saved from demolition by Curtis and Norma Grace, who opened it as a restaurant in 1974. Rescue of this important landmark spearheaded restoration in a 30-block area; Lower Town Historic District was placed on The National Register in 1982.

At the Ninth Street House, restored to its original Victorian elegance, dark woodwork, sweeping stairs, and stained and beveled glass are enhanced by antiques of the period, including an 1865 Steinway played on weekend nights. Beneath decorative mantels in each dining room, fires on cool evenings add to the candlelit intimacy, and the enclosed piazza is a year-round "Garden Room."

"Classic Southern Cooking" at The Ninth Street House showcases the creative genius of owner/chef Curtis Grace in frequently changing menus. Fresh seafoods, prime rib, and lamb are constants, other entrées vary daily, and a "Little Menu" offers lighter fare Tuesday through Thursday.

Lunch includes soup, unusual sandwiches, California Chicken Salad—shredded chicken breast with grapes and almonds, topped with a curry dressing—an enormous Chef's Salad, and a Daily Special.

Breads, dressings, and ice creams are homemade, as are marvelous desserts that frequently feature crisp pastry, fresh fruit, and gobs of whipped cream. The iced tea, a house secret, has been called "the best in the world!"

The Ninth Street House, 323 Ninth Street, is open Tuesday through Saturday. Lunch is 11 a.m. to 2 p.m.; dinner is 6 to 8:30 p.m. (502)442-9019. All beverages are available, dress is informal, and reservations are suggested. DC,MC,V. ($$)

NINTH STREET TOMATO SOUP SPICE CAKE**

1 packaged	1/4 cup water
spice cake mix	1/2 cup raisins
10-ounce can	1/2 cup chopped pecans
condensed tomato soup	Golden Butter Frosting

Prepare cake mix according to package directions, using soup and water as liquid. Stir in raisins and pecans. Pour into 2 greased, lightly floured 8" round pans and bake at 325 degrees 30 to 35 minutes. Cool in pans 10 minutes; remove from pans and cool.

For frosting: beat together 1/2 cup softened butter, 1 egg yolk, 2 Tablespoons buttermilk, and 1/2 teaspoon vanilla, gradually adding 3 cups powdered sugar. Frost completely cooled cake. Serves 12.

NINTH STREET HOUSE VEGETABLE PIE***

10-inch	1/4 teaspoon
baked pie shell	black pepper
3 to 4 Tablespoons butter	Dash garlic salt
1 pound fresh	1 tomato, sliced
mushrooms, sliced	1 cup mayonnaise
1 onion, sliced	1 cup grated
2 zucchini or	Mozzarella cheese
yellow squash, sliced	
1 green pepper, sliced	
1 teaspoon salt	

In skillet, melt butter and sauté vegetables until crisp. Drain well and season. Place tomato slices in bottom of pie shell; add vegetables. Mix mayonnaise with cheese and spead on top. Bake 45 minutes to 1 hour at 325 degrees. Serves 6.

NINTH STREET
CHICKEN IN PHYLLO**

3/4 cup chopped
  green onions and tops
3/4 cup mayonnaise
3 Tablespoons
  lemon juice
3 small cloves garlic,
  minced
1/2 teaspoon dry tarragon

12 chicken breast halves,
  skinned and boned
Salt and pepper
24 sheets phyllo dough
2/3 cup melted butter
Grated Parmesan cheese
Mornay Sauce*

In bowl, mix first 5 ingredients. Set aside. Season chicken. Brush 2 phyllo sheets with butter. Dip 1 breast into mayonnaise mixture, place on sheet, top with second sheet, and wrap, envelope-style. Brush top with butter and sprinkle with cheese. Repeat with each breast. Place in ungreased pan and bake at 375 degrees 30 minutes. Serve with Mornay Sauce. Serves 12.

*Most general cookbooks have a recipe for this classic sauce.

NINTH STREET HOUSE
DOTTIE'S SPINACH SALAD**

10 ounces fresh spinach,
  washed, drained,
  and torn
12-ounce carton
  cottage cheese, rinsed
1/2 cup chopped pecans
1/2 cup sour cream

1/4 cup sugar
2 Tablespoons vinegar
2 Tablespoons
  horseradish
1/2 teaspoon dry mustard
1/4 teaspoon salt

In large bowl, combine first three ingredients . In smaller bowl, mix remaining ingredients, then combine with spinach mixture. Serves 4.

Note: Curtis often garnishes this with fresh strawberries.

THE HAPPY HOUSE
Mayfield

In 1816, General Andrew Jackson and Governor Isaac Shelby of Kentucky were commissioned by the United States Government to treat with the Chickasaw Indian Nation for a tract of land. After two years of negotiation, they were successful, and "The Jackson Purchase," including all land between the Tennessee and Mississippi rivers, from the Ohio River to the northern Boundary of Mississippi, was added to the states of Kentucky and Tennessee.

Eight counties in southwestern Kentucky came out of the purchase, and settlement began as soon as the Indians migrated to Mississippi.

Near the center of the Kentucky segment of The Purchase is Mayfield, county seat of Graves County, and sometimes called the "Hub of the Purchase." It was settled in 1819 by John Anderson, and was first peopled by Carolinians, later by those who flatboated down the Ohio to Paducah, then traveled overland.

Mayfield has produced many enterprising citizens— an example is Howard D. Happy, known in Mayfield as "the only man who started a business without borrowing a dime."

Happy, a brilliant student, was equipped to become an attorney in 1914 at the age of 19, but was too young to take the bar. Working as a court reporter, he was hired by Royal Typewriter as a field representative in Western Kentucky and Tennessee; he sold his first consignment of three typewriters, and was sent five; he sold those, and was a dealer by 1916. Adding other business machines to his stock, he became the largest office equipment dealer in Western Kentucky, with branches in Paducah and Hopkinsville.

His home, a two-story Colonial Revival in native brown stone, was designed for gracious living by his wife, and continues the tradition of elegant entertaining as The Happy House Restaurant. Opened in 1985 by Pauline Russelberg, The Happy House is decorated in warm rose, ivory, and blue, each room with its own bright, fresh atmosphere. It provides food that is delicious, satisfying, and attractive.

Lunch choices include homemade soups, crisp salads (one combination is spinach, mushrooms, oranges and bacon) unusual sandwiches, and quiches, with special attention to diet- and health-conscious guests.

The dinner specialty is carefully prepared prime rib, plus steaks, two kinds of seafood daily, chicken entrées, and "different" fresh vegetables. All breads, salad dressings, and desserts are homemade. Especially memorable are Frozen Strawberry Parfait, chess and fudge pies, and rich, fudgey, well-named Miracle Pie.

The Happy House, 236 North 8th Street, Mayfield, is on a one-way street southbound, easily located from the north, but requiring a bit of maneuvering from the south. It is open for lunch 11 a.m. to 2 p.m., Tuesday through Saturday, and for dinner 6 to 10 p.m., Friday and Saturday. It is closed the first week in April. (502)247-5743. Dress is casual, and no charge cards are accepted; reservations are requested for groups of 6 or more. It is busiest during Mayfest, the first week in May. ($$)

HAPPY HOUSE COPENHAGEN SANDWICH

For each sandwich:
2 slices rye bread
1 slice deli turkey
1 leaf lettuce,
  washed and drained

2 slices tomato
2 green onions,
  with tops, chopped
Spinach dressing

Place bread slices on plate, side by side. Top with turkey, lettuce, and tomato, and sprinkle with green onions. Place a dollop of dressing on top.

For dressing: place 1 cup chopped spinach and 1 cup Hellman's™ (no substitute) mayonnaise in blender and blend thoroughly. Yields enough for several sandwiches.

HAPPY HOUSE
LOW CALORIE HEALTH SANDWICH

For each sandwich:
1 English muffin or
  bagel, halved crosswise
1/2 slice deli turkey

1 large mushroom, sliced
3 slices apple, peel on
1 green onion, chopped
Red wine vinegar

Place muffin or bagel on plate open-faced. Layer with turkey, mushrooms, and apples. Serve onion on the side, with a small container of red wine vinegar.

HAPPY HOUSE ICE CREAM PIE

Chocolate cookie crumb
  crust
1 pint butter pecan
  ice cream, softened
1 cup fudge topping
  (divided)

1 Heath Bar™ candy bar,
  chopped
1 pint coffee ice cream,
  softened
Whipped cream

In prepared crust, spread butter pecan ice cream; top with 3/4 cup fudge topping, sprinkle with Heath Bar™ pieces, and spread coffee ice cream on top. Freeze pie until hard. To serve, cut into wedges, top with whipped cream, and drizzle with remaining fudge topping.

INDEX TO RESTAURANTS

INDEX TO RECIPES

Buttermilk Coconut Pie, The Main Street House, 67
Buttermilk Pound Cake with Lemon Glaze, Holly Hill Inn, 75
Cheesecake, Mariah's 1818, 163
Cherry Cobbler, The Depot, 19
Chocolate Bread, Parisian Pantry, 147
Date Fingers, Two Thirteen on Main, 83
Date Nut Bread, deSha's, 47
Double Layer Chocolate Ganache, Dudley's, 51
Engine House Brownies, The Engine House Deli, 27
Frozen Banana Salad, Academy Inn, 70
Frozen Fruit Salad, The Tea Leaf, 87
Hot Fudge Cake, Back Home, 155
Ice Cream Pie, The Happy House, 199
Irish Brownie, The Old House, 139
Lemon Bread, The Shaker Village of Pleasant Hill, 91
Lemon Ice Box Pie, deSha's, 47
Old Talbott Tavern Pie, Old Talbott Tavern, 119
Orange Ice Box Cookies, Duncan Tavern, 31
Peanut Butter Pie, The Main Street House, 67
Pecan Macaroons, Duncan Tavern, 31
Pink Lemonade Pie, The Carrollton Inn, 103
Pumpkin Cheese Roll, Academy Inn, 71
Pumpkin-Chip Muffins, The Tea Leaf, 87
Strawberry Cream Pie, The Courthouse Café, 15
Strawberry Dessert, The Old House, 139
Toll House Pie, Colby's, 175
Tomato Soup Spice Cake, The Ninth Street House, 194
Tom's Delicious Peach Cobbler, Back Home, 155
"Twice Baked" Cheesecake, Woodbury House, 171

FRUITS
Apple Brown Betty, Beaumont Inn, 95
Frozen Banana Salad, Academy Inn, 70
Frozen Fruit Salad, The Tea Leaf, 87
Strawberry Shortcake (drink), Bartholomew's, 187
Pineapple au Gratin, Back Home, 155
Pink Strawberry Soup, Holly Hill Inn, 74
Spicy Peach Salad, Two Thirteen on Main, 82
Strawberry Dessert, The Old House, 139
Strawberry Cream Pie, The Courthouse Café, 15
Tom's Delicious Peach Cobbler, Back Home, 155

MAIN DISHES
Bean Soup, Our Best Restaurant, 111
Bean Soup, Wolf's Tavern, 182
Bean Soup, Woodbury House, 170
Cajun Chicken, The Carrollton Inn, 103
California Chicken Salad, Mariah's 1818, 162

Dottie's Spinach Salad, The Ninth Street House, 195
Engine House Dressing, The Engine House Deli, 27
Frozen Banana Salad, Academy Inn, 70
Frozen Fruit Salad, The Tea Leaf, 87
Grilled Chicken Salad, The Parakeet Café, 166
Grilled Heartland Vegetable Salad, Seelbach Hotel, 130
Grilled Shrimp and Spinach Salad, Trotters, 179
Hot Bacon Dressing, Trotters, 179
Kentucky Limestone Salad, The Brown Hotel, 135
Kentucky Style Hot German Potato Salad, Iron Kettle, 191
Niçoise Salad, The Mike Fink, 39
Orange Dressing (for fruit), Colby's, 174
Shrimp Salad, John E's, 127
Spicy Peach Salad, Two Thirteen on Main, 82
Spinach Salad with Carpaccio of Tenderloin, Wheeler's Roadhouse, 143
Summer Slaw, Woodbury House, 170
Warm Brie Salad, Train Station Restaurant, 115
White House Dressing, Beaumont Inn, 94

SANDWICHES
Copenhagen Sandwich, The Happy House, 198
Low Calorie Health Sandwich, The Happy House, 199
"Original" Hot Brown Sandwich, The Brown Hotel, 134

SAUCES
Bourbon Sauce for Biscuit Pudding, Science Hill Inn, 107
Currant Sauce for Pork Loin, Uptown Chatter, 78
Orange Dressing (for fruit), Colby's, 174
Tomato Basil Cream, The Parakeet Café, 167
Wellington Sauce for Supremes of Chicken Wellington, La Taberna, 123
Whiskey Sauce for Bread Pudding, The Mansion at Griffin Gate, 59

SEAFOODS AND FRESH WATER FISH
Coconut Fried Shrimp, The Main Street House, 66
Fish Fillets Wellington, Merrick Inn, 62
Fish Fritters, Beehive Tavern, 23
Grilled Shrimp and Spinach Salad, Trotters, 179
Maryland Crab Cakes with Ginger Rémoulade, Deitrich's in the Crescent, 150
Mushroom Clam Bisque, Rick's City Café, 98
Seafood Chowder, The Carrollton Inn, 102
Shrinp and Crab Fritters, Train Station Restaurant, 114
Shrimp Dijon, The Mansion at Griffin Gate, 58
Shrimp Louisiane, Bartholomew's, 186
Shrimp Salad, John E's, 127
Shrimp Scampi, The Main Street House, 67
Shrimp Scampi, The Mike Fink, 38

SOUPS

Asparagus and Jalapeño Pepper Cheese Soup, Wheeler's Roadhouse, 142

Bean Soup, Our Best Restaurant, 111

Bean Soup, Wolf's Tavern, 182

Bean Soup, Woodbury House, 170

Broccoli Cheese Soup, Mariah's 1818, 162

Carrot Soup Au Crème, La Taberna, 122

Chicken and Rice Soup, Colby's, 175

Cream of Broccoli Soup, The Depot, 18

Cream of Pimiento Soup, Boone Tavern, 34

Cream of Tomato Soup, Science Hill Inn, 106

Cuban Black Bean Soup, Beehive Tavern, 22

Herbed Tomato Soup, Courthouse Café, 14

Mixed Bean Soup, Dudley's, 50

Mushroom Clam Bisque, Rick's City Café, 98

Pink Strawberry Soup, Holly Hill Inn, 74

Seafood Chowder, The Carrollton Inn, 102

Tomato Bisque with Croutons, Merrick Inn, 63

VEGETABLES

Asparagus Salad, Two Thirteen on Main, 83

Brussels Sprouts and Carrots with Hot Bacon Dressing, The Whistle Stop, 159

Carrot Soufflé, The Old House, 138

Corn Pudding, The Whistle Stop, 159

Kentucky Style Hot German Potato Salad, The Iron Kettle, 191

Kraut Casserole, The Iron Kettle, 191

Mixed Greens, Dee Felice Café, 43

Mushrooms Imperiale, John E's, 126

Potato Casserole, Uptown Chatter, 79

Stuffed Artichoke Hearts Philadelphia, Trotters, 178

Sweet Potato Casserole, deSha's, 46

Sweet Potato Casserole, The Iron Kettle, 190

Sweet Potato Soufflé, Academy Inn, 71

Vegetable Pie, The Ninth Street House, 194

Zucchini Charlotte, Beaumont Inn, 95